XLI
2 H 48

in print
at $15.95
84

INVESTING FOR PROFIT
IN THE EIGHTIES

Other books by Alfred L. Malabre, Jr.

UNDERSTANDING THE ECONOMY:
For People Who Can't Stand Economics

AMERICA'S DILEMMA:
Jobs vs. Prices

INVESTING FOR PROFIT IN THE EIGHTIES

The Business Cycle System

Alfred L. Malabre, Jr.

Doubleday & Co., Inc.
Garden City, New York
1982

In Loving Memory of Emma Hovland

Excerpts from "How to Keep the IRS Off Your Back" from the March 24, 1980, issue of *U.S. News & World Report*, copyright © 1980 by U.S. News & World Report. Reprinted by permission.

Library of Congress Cataloging in Publication Data

Malabre, Alfred L.
   Investing for profit in the eighties.

   Includes index.
   1. Investments—United States—Handbooks, manuals, etc.
I. Title.
HG4921.M32   332.6′78   80–2971
ISBN: 0-385-17047-5

Copyright © 1982 by Alfred L. Malabre, Jr.

All Rights Reserved
Printed in the United States of America
First Edition

Contents

1. Do It Yourself! — 1
2. Learning to Do It Myself — 6
3. Don't Follow the Leaders — 15
4. Mavericks — 23
5. Nowhere to Turn — 37
6. On My Own — 49
7. Longer Trends — 59
8. Seeing the Cycle — 77
9. Keeping Ahead of the Cycle — 84
10. Riding the Stock Market — 103
11. Picking Stocks — 113
12. A Word of Warning — 124
13. Fixed-income Investing — 140
14. Tangibles — 157
15. Putting It Together — 174
16. Loose Ends — 186
    Index — 203

INVESTING FOR PROFIT
IN THE EIGHTIES

1.
Do It Yourself!

THE CHANCES ARE THAT YOU QUALIFY AS AN INVESTOR. NEVER mind that you're not rich. Or that your income is only average or perhaps below average. Or that you own just a few shares of stock. Or that your savings account is below five digits.

Do you own a home? Or partake in a company retirement program? Or have life insurance? Or, under the Reagan administration's new tax rules, have an Individual Retirement Account that you're trying to manage yourself?

Mr. Webster defines an investor as anyone who commits money in order to earn financial benefits in the future.

Most adult Americans, whether they realize it or not, are investors.

This book is for the broad spectrum of investors, big and little and in between. It aims as well at people who may have no money now for investing but hope to have some someday. And it offers a straightforward technique of investing that can be applied in just about any sort of economic weather.

If you happen, as most of us do, to fall within the less-than-big-investor category, consider this:

A 1980 study by the United States Trust Co., the Wall Street bank, estimates there are about 575,000 millionaires in America, up from 180,000 as recently as 1972. That means approximately one of roughly every 140 American households is worth at least $1 million.

And, of course, for each of these, many others approach millionaire status, with a personal worth in the hundreds of thousands of dollars.

New York State alone, the national leader in this regard, boasts more than 56,000 millionaires. Other states with at least 20,000 millionaires include California, Illinois, Ohio, Florida, New Jersey, Indiana, Idaho, Wisconsin, Minnesota, and Texas.

A startling statistic: Twenty-seven of every 1,000 residents of Idaho, where the value of land has soared, are worth at least $1 million.

Many of these wealthy individuals engage high-priced investment managers to try to safeguard their fortunes. That is their obvious right. However, this book grows out of a conviction, firmly held and painfully acquired, that you don't need to—in fact, you probably shouldn't—go out and hire the advice of expensive money managers to achieve investment success and safety. And that applies even if you are fortunate enough to be among America's 575,000 millionaires.

A Set of Rules

You will find, on the pages that follow, that sensible investing can be accomplished by adhering to simple rules. You'll probably make no stock-market killings through what's offered on these pages. But neither will you have to worry about financial wipeouts.

The main lesson:

Remember that there's a great big economy out there, and how it behaves can influence mightily how your particular investments will behave. A lot of very sophisticated money managers continually forget that central fact.

Another rule:

Stick to basics. They are easy to pick out and understand.

Another rule:
Be patient, very patient—yet always ready to make a change.
Summing up:
You *can* do it yourself—and you most probably *should* do it yourself.

You will see on these pages precisely why, if you value your wherewithal, you had better start doing it yourself.

And that applies whether your wherewithal amounts to $10,000, or $100,000, or $1,000,000.

If you're looking for the latest trick way to trade soybeans or stock options or currency futures, this isn't your book. You will find little here that many Wall Streeters would regard as a sophisticated investment technique.

However, you will find a great deal of simple common sense that all too often gets neglected by supposedly sophisticated investment professionals.

My skepticism about the professionals may sound a bit strange coming, as it does, from someone who has labored in the heart of the nation's investment community—the Wall Street area—for about a quarter of a century. But it's precisely because I've observed the investment scene for so long that I've grown so dubious about the advice dished out there.

As the saying goes, if you get too close to the trees, you won't be able to spot the forest. The "forest" that habitually is missed by many sophisticated folk who dish out investment advice is the American economy.

All too often, the focus is only on the "trees":

What happened to the money supply last week? What did the consumer price index do last month? Did General Motors change its dividend yesterday? What's the new report from Detroit on car sales? What was in the message from the White House last night? What's the morning fixing on the price of gold? How did the new Bell Telephone bond issue sell yesterday? How much is the steel union demanding?

As a business writer, I'm paid to keep a close tab on such matters. For you, following all the economic "trees" most likely isn't very enticing. Who can blame you? Believe me, to do so involves day-by-day, even hour-by-hour, monitoring of the news that few individuals could afford to do, or, indeed, would care to tie up their time attempting to do.

Don't feel left out if you don't—can't—monitor all the "trees." Feel fortunate. I'll argue, in fact, that such vigilance is dangerous to the extent that it draws your attention away from the "forest."

You'll see in this book that gaining a clear insight into the nature of the American economy and following its broad behavior from month to month and from year to year can be a simple exercise. And you will find that making the additional connection—relating the economy's behavior to a sensible investment strategy—entails a remarkably simple, straightforward procedure.

You will come to understand, I believe, why it's possible to regard the economy as a roller coaster, steeply on the rise, then leveling out, dropping in frightening fashion, repeating the cycle. Like a roller coaster, the economy is constantly on the move. And the approximate motion, like a roller-coaster ride, can be anticipated.

There will be surprises. But you can generally muster a pretty good idea of what will be coming next along the track. You may not pinpoint the timing or extent of the ups and downs exactly right. However, if you keep your eyes open, in all probability you won't be expecting, say, a sudden drop just when a sudden climb is getting under way.

For All Seasons

In ensuing chapters, you will observe repeated instances of how investment professionals have failed investors—including me. You will learn a do-it-yourself investment technique not just for good business years or bad business years or for times of high inflation. It will be for all seasons.

What if the coming years turn out to be good ones for the

economy, instead of bad ones as so many Cassandras have been warning? What if inflation simmers down and doesn't rekindle?

Inflation has been with us for much of the post-World War II era. But no one should expect the future to be a carbon copy of the past. It never is. Did you know that the country's general price level was higher in the mid-1860s than in the mid-1940s?

This book assumes that the investment climate can change dramatically. Indeed, it assumes that it's in constant flux. Inflation heats up, inflation cools down. Employment grows, employment shrivels. Profits soar, profits plunge. Inventories pile up, shortages develop.

Economists call it the business cycle. In their jargon, the economy inevitably is in one of the following phases:

1. Recovery from a recession.
2. Expansion to a new business-cycle peak (call it a boom if things get overheated and prices go wild).
3. Recession (or depression if things get bad enough).

Perhaps inflation will rage during the next five years, perhaps not. Armed with an understanding of the business cycle, you will be ready for either eventuality.

You will see an investment strategy geared—first, last, and always—to the business cycle. Few books about investing even take note of the business cycle, much less attempt to understand it and help individuals to set their investment technique accordingly.

You will gain an appreciation of the economy's ups and downs, see how to anticipate them, and learn how to tailor your investment moves to them. You will be shown the tools of analysis that I've used as a business columnist to inform readers where the economy stands and where it's likely to go.

2.
Learning to Do It Myself

AVON PRODUCTS INC. IS THE WORLD'S LARGEST MANUFACTURER OF cosmetics and toiletries. It markets its wares from door to door, employing over 1 million sales people worldwide. It does business in over two dozen countries, besides the United States.

Avon also happens to be a company in which our family for a very brief time had a very small investment. The story of how we got into the Avon investment, and then what happened, provides a useful starting point—a warning, if you will—for anyone who has a little savings and an itch to invest them in corporate America. In a word, the message is:

Beware!

The story of our brief investment in Avon begins in the early months of 1972. Until that time, I had for many years managed with sporadic success to oversee my family's less-than-Brobdingnagian portfolio. The corporate names on our modest list, I am sure, will not be unfamiliar to those of you with at least a passing interest in the stock market—such stolid enterprises as Continental Oil Co., recently acquired by Du Pont, the chemicals giant, and now called Conoco Inc.; American Telephone & Telegraph Co.; Wisconsin Electric Power; Standard Oil of California; American Metal Climax Inc., now known as

Amax Inc.; and Standard Oil of New Jersey, now called Exxon Corp.

Even in 1972 these corporations were hardly fledgling outfits. Huge then, they are huger still today. Then or now, none surely could be characterized as a diamond in the rough, undiscovered, with a potential in future years to make the brave investor rich.

They were, as I say, stolid—in no way glamorous but, it seemed to me, reasonably secure, generating a decent amount of dividends for stockholders every quarter. Each had occupied a significant spot in our small portfolio for a while, and I fully imagined in early 1972 that each would continue to be an investment holding for a good while longer.

But this was not to be. In the early weeks of 1972, I discovered to my delight that my employer intended to transfer me from a long-standing editorial assignment in New York City to London, where I would be undertaking an assignment of indefinite duration involving frequent travel, not only around the United Kingdom, but up and down and across Western Europe, occasionally into the European Communist countries and Russia and, very infrequently, through the Middle East and Africa.

In the frenetic days before departing New York for London, a thousand and one decisions had of course to be made—talks with moving men, haggling with travel agents, negotiating with real-estate brokers, waiting at the passport office, conferring at the post office, seeking the advice of bankers.

Especially seeking the advice of bankers.

Anyone who has lived for any time abroad on an American salary will surely know how important it is to have a bank knowledgeable, for instance, in foreign-exchange matters, preferably one with branches in key cities abroad.

Enter Citibank

I had—fortunately, it then seemed—just such a bank: Citibank, or as it called itself in those somewhat more elegant years, First

National City Bank of New York. It maintained large branches not only in London but also in an assortment of other foreign cities that I would no doubt be passing through from time to time in my newspaper travels. Through a series of pleasant conferences with Citibank people in the New York headquarters on Park Avenue, arrangements were carefully made for me to obtain various banking conveniences, including of course a checking account, at the organization's large West End of London branch, just off Berkeley Square.

One other matter occurred to me, as I talked with the bank's people in New York. I would be departing for London in mid-June, I explained, and beyond that point would frequently be on the road and out of touch. Our family happened to have a small portfolio of stocks, on which I had recently been keeping an eye. I was a bit concerned, I related, about being able to devote sufficient attention to this nest egg once on the go abroad. Did they have any suggestion?

Indeed, they said, they did have. For a reasonable fee, I was informed, the bank would not only take safe custody in New York of our few securities while I was abroad, but the bank would "manage" them. I was aware that such services had long existed at major New York-based banks. The usual procedure, I knew, involved a bank official periodically scrutinizing a client's portfolio and then possibly suggesting some change or other—for example, selling XXX shares of General Motors and with the proceeds purchasing YYY shares of International Business Machines or whatever. The client would then, after weighing the proposal, say yes or no.

This was approximately the arrangement suggested by the Citibank people. But not exactly. Because of the unusual circumstances of the arrangement with me—a client thousands of miles away from the bank's home investment base and, more often than not, on the distant road—it was suggested, indeed it was urged, that I allow Citibank something called "discretion" over the portfolio. There often might not be time to await my approval from abroad, it was noted, when a prompt portfolio change seemed appropriate.

The additional service would cost me a moderately higher fee. But I was warned that undue delay in making a suggested change from one stock, deemed unsuitable, to another, deemed attractive to buy promptly, could spell investment disaster.

Of course the idea made wonderful good sense. And of course I consented, almost gratefully, handing over to Citibank this "discretionary" power—the authority to juggle our family portfolio held in the bank's custody in New York, without my prior approval or even my foreknowledge, of any planned changes.

I confess that for a brief moment I felt a twinge of concern that perhaps I should retain control even if that meant considerable delay in executing recommended portfolio changes. However, the two Citibank gentlemen who were to assume the discretionary responsibility impressed me greatly as cautious, prudent, sober to the point of somberness, in all ways perspicacious.

Surely, I told myself, I would be in good hands. And so the agreement was sealed and I turned to other pressing details in preparation for our June departure to London. One less responsibility, I assumed, now would weigh upon my already overburdened shoulders.

There was precious little time in our first few weeks in London for any daily perusal of how the Dow Jones industrial stock average might be behaving back in New York, much less for keeping a tab on the ups and downs of the individual stocks that we had left behind under the discretionary care of the gentlemen at Citibank. Far from my mind was any thought, worried or otherwise, about what if anything might be happening to the portfolio.

In fact, back at the Park Avenue headquarters of Citibank a great deal was happening. The bankers there not only had discretionary power over our investments, but, as I was soon to discover, were furiously exercising it.

Only as the London summer, a typically cold, dank affair, moved toward fall did I become gradually aware, through the mail, of what was happening back in New York. Only months later, after I had returned there to take up another job for the paper, unexpectedly cutting short the London assignment, was I able to piece together the extent of the portfolio changes undertaken during my absence.

Sold during that dreary London summer were all the aforementioned stolid holdings—Continental Oil at $26.125 a share, Wisconsin Electric Power at $21.75, American Telephone at $41.875, Standard Oil of New Jersey at $76, Standard Oil of California at $59.125 and American Metal Climax at $28.875.

And purchased in their stead for our nest-egg list during our absence were an assortment of new names—Sears, Roebuck & Co. at $110 a share, Continental Telephone Corp. at $20.50, International Business Machines at $398, Southland Corp. at $40, and, never to be forgotten, Avon Products at $119.

I recognized without undue deliberation that the changes undertaken by Citibank would reduce our dividends. At the time, the average annual dividend yield was 1.1 percent a share on the Avon stock, 0.7 percent on Southland, 1.4 percent on IBM, 3.7 percent on Continental Telephone, and 1.4 percent on Sears Roebuck. These compared with yields of 4.9 percent on Continental Oil and on Standard Oil of New Jersey, 6 percent on American Telephone, 6.6 percent on Wisconsin Electric Power, and 4.7 percent on American Metal Climax.

However, it was explained to me, our apparent loss in dividend earnings would in the long run be more than offset by the sustained "growth"—that, I discovered, was a favorite word of our Citibank advisers—anticipated for our new holdings. These newcomers to our portfolio, we were assured, possessed a dynamism that would surely carry them safely through economic storms that might from time to time develop in the future. In short, our portfolio was pronounced a good deal stronger for the switching.

I wondered.

No More Discretion

Uneasily, I pondered the reduced amounts in our dividend checks. Warily, I noted that whatever future "growth" might be in store for our new investments, little of it seemed to be translating into higher prices for the particular securities. Weeks passed. The chores of resettling in New York finally behind us, I decided—politely, with no hint of acrimony—to inform my banker friends that I wished to take back "discretion" over the portfolio. There was no problem. A simple letter sufficed to complete the change.

In the early months of 1973, for reasons that will presently be explained, I decided to do some portfolio switching myself. Most of the sales were made in May. The Sears was unloaded at $98 a share, a loss of $12 a share. The Southland was sold at $31, about $9 under cost. The others, in retrospect miraculously, were sold at a profit—Continental Telephone at $22.875, up $2.375 from our cost, IBM at $406.75, up $8.75, and Avon at $127.25, up—*mirabile dictu*—$8.25.

In May of 1973 the American economy was still expanding briskly, as it had been since late in 1970. The oil embargo imposed by the Arab countries in the fall of 1973 and the subsequent series of sharp oil price increases lay in the future.

So did the onset of what was to become, up to that time, the most severe American business slump since the 1930s, the recession of 1973–75. That downturn began in November of 1973 and kept deepening until March of 1975; it amounted to nearly a year and a half of economic misery. As usual before downphases of the American business cycle, the stock market began slipping several months before the recession set in. Again typically, the stock market then started recovering shortly before the recession ended. Before the stock-market turnaround, of course, the prices of most shares declined sharply, some far more steeply than others. Among the most severely hit, as it happened, were the very securities that I had finally mustered up the initiative to sell in May.

Most stocks reached their recessionary low points during

1974. In December of that year, the Standard & Poor's index of 500 common stocks, for example, stood at 67.07, some 43 percent below its reading in January of 1973. The index closely approximates the average movement of all stocks listed on the New York Stock Exchange. The price of each of the 500 component stocks is weighted by the number of shares outstanding, and the aggregate market value is expressed in terms of the average market value in the base period, which happens to be 1941–43. The 1941–43 average is taken to be 10, so that an index reading of, say, 20 would indicate a doubling of market value over the base figure.

Four groups comprise the index: 400 industrial stocks, 40 public utilities, 20 transportation companies and 40 financial concerns. Each stock in the index represents a viable enterprise, representative of the industry to which it is assigned. Its price movements in general must be responsive to changes in industry affairs. Selection of stocks for addition to or removal from the index is the decision of Standard & Poor's.

That 43 percent decline in the index, as painful as it may appear, was mild alongside the plunge endured by some of our erstwhile "growth" stocks. During 1974 Sears, Roebuck sank to a low of $41.50 a share, Continental Telephone to $9.25, Southland to $13.25, and IBM to $150.50, a 53 percent decline even with a five-for-four split of the stock. The collapse in Avon, to $18.625 a share, works out to a decline of more than 85 percent from the May sale level.

To be sure, some of the securities sold by Citibank during the summer of 1972 fell as well during 1974. However, by comparison, the declines were mild. And, in some cases, prices actually rose.

Continental Oil's low for the year 1974 was $29 a share, actually an increase from the price at which the stock had been sold by Citibank in 1972. Wisconsin Electric Power's 1974 low was $16 a share; American Telephone's, $39.625; Exxon's, $54.875; Standard Oil of California's, $40.25, allowing for a two-for-one split of the stock; and American Metal Climax's, $30.25.

LEARNING TO DO IT MYSELF

The sales that I undertook in May of 1973 quite obviously enabled us, as things turned out, to escape a very large amount of immediate financial pain. (I will take up later what I did with the proceeds of those sales and the reasoning that prompted my highly unconventional course of action.)

What about the longer term?

The gentlemen at Citibank had justified their maneuvers on the ground that "growth" over the long haul was the goal. While conceding that what constitutes the long haul for one individual may seem only short-term for another, I suggest that close to a decade is long enough for all but the Methuselahs of the investment community. It certainly seems time enough to assess the success or failure of a particular stock pick.

Accordingly, let us have a look at where the securities that I unloaded in May of 1973 stood in mid-February of 1980, around the start of a new decade.

Sears, Roebuck was selling at $17.25 a share. Even taking into account a two-for-one-stock split in 1977, this amounted to far less than I had paid for the stock, under Citibank's guidance, back in the summer of 1972. Continental Telephone was selling at $14.25 a share, also well below the 1972 price. IBM was selling at $67.625, again less than the 1972 price despite the aforementioned five-for-four split and another split of four-for-one in 1979. Southland was selling at $27.125 a share, well below the 1972 price. And Avon, still floundering, was up only to $35.125, far, far below the 1972 purchase price.

Now let's take a further glance at the prices in mid-February of 1980 of stocks sold by Citibank during that long-ago London summer.

Continental Oil was selling at $55.375 a share, and the stock had split two-for-one in 1976; thus, on a 1972 basis, it was selling more than $110 a share, or more than four times the price at which it had been sold by Citibank in 1972. Exxon was selling at $64 a share, and that stock too had been split two-for-one in 1976; in 1972 terms, Exxon was selling at $128 a share. Standard Oil of California was selling at $70.50 a share; it too had split two-for-one in 1973, so that in 1972 terms it was selling at $141 a share. Amax was selling $54.625 a share, and the stock had split three-for-two in 1979; again, this represented a sharp increase over the price at which the stock had been sold in 1972. Wisconsin Electric Power was selling at $20.125 a share, approximately the same level at which it was sold in 1972; however, the dividend was at an annual rate of $2.47 a share, up sharply from $1.54 a share in 1972.

The numbers add up to a sorry commentary on the investment advice and, for us, a narrow escape from a financial debacle.

3.
Don't Follow the Leaders

IN THE SPRING OF 1973 I WAS NOT EXACTLY A NEOPHYTE WANdering naïvely within the environs of Wall Street. I had already covered the general field of investment and finance in the United States and for several brief intervals overseas for more than fifteen years. I had been news editor of *The Wall Street Journal*, with special responsibility for the paper's business and economic coverage, for four years. I had been writing the paper's front page "Outlook" column, which appears each Monday, for nearly a decade. I most certainly understood the difference between, say, a share of stock and a bond certificate, and a good deal more than that. I had written countless articles on countless facets of investing.

Notwithstanding, my experience with the Citibank bankers during that summer in 1972—my brush with Avon and the other nearly disastrous investments noted in the previous chapter—taught me quite a number of things about the business of looking after one's savings that I had not managed really to pick up and assimilate during all those years on the job.

The overriding lesson, of course, was coming clear to me: Don't blindly trust—as I briefly did—the big-name professionals to be your investment guardians.

Mr. Webster tells us that the word "establishment" may be defined as the social, economic, or political leaders of an established order of society. By that definition, there can be little question that Citibank must rank as a prominent member of the country's economic establishment, along with a select assortment of other large financial institutions, many of them based like Citibank in Manhattan. What Mr. Webster does not tell us is how it was possible for a "leader" in the country's economic establishment to study a stock like Avon in 1972 and conclude that it should be bought for the modest portfolio of a distant, unavailable client of modest income.

David N. Dreman is an independent investment manager who has achieved considerable success over the years by eschewing securities whose price tags, in terms of per-share earnings, appear relatively high. Writing in a December 1979 issue of *Barron's,* the national business and financial weekly published by Dow Jones & Co., Mr. Dreman had this to say about Avon:

"Sometimes a few of the more naive investors—such as large institutions—have gotten carried away with the growth theory. During . . . 1971–1973, Avon commanded a higher market value than the entire U.S. steel industry. . . ."

Not bad for a company selling cosmetics door to door. But hardly a realistic assessment of its value. Yet, as I painfully learned firsthand, that was the sort of price that the people at Citibank were willing to pay for Avon shares in 1972.

Parenthetically, I should explain that there are many ways to assess the "value" of a particular stock. A stock may indeed be "valued" at more than a whole industry. You can multiply the stock's market price on, say, the New York Stock Exchange by the number of shares outstanding. Then you can go through the same procedure for all stocks of companies in the industry in question and add up the totals. Then you can compare the single stock's "value" with the industry's "value."

This is not, however, a method recommended for a do-it-yourself investor. A simpler technique—and in my view a sounder one—is to focus on what analysts call a stock's "price-earnings ratio." This is nothing more than the ratio of a stock's per-share price to its per-share earnings. If XYZ Corp. is selling at $100 a share and it has earned $10 in the past year, its price-earnings ratio is 10. To make things extra easy, many newspapers list stocks' price-earnings ratios on a daily basis, as a part of the stock-quote tables on the financial pages. There is no single "appropriate" price-earnings level for a stock. The ratio will vary from company to company, from industry to industry, from recession to recovery, even from business-cycle sequence to business-cycle sequence. As a general rule, stocks in industries perceived to have especially good long-term prospects carry relatively high price-earnings ratios, for obvious reasons, and stocks in troubled or declining industries, just as obviously, tend to have relatively low ratios.

Not Just Citibank

If my experience at the hands of Citibank were unique, one might deem my distrust of the economic establishment excessive. Unhappily, my experience is in no way unique. As Mr. Dreman suggests, Avon was a favorite of the investment managers of *most* major banks during the period, not simply of Citibank. Indeed, establishment demand for Avon and several dozen other "growth" stocks led to a two-tier stock market in the early 1970s—a first tier composed of stocks with sky-high price tags, in terms of earnings, and a second tier of stocks with sharply lower price-to-earnings levels. The first-tier group was occasionally referred to along Wall Street as the "vestal virgins," because, in the view of skeptics, such stocks with their lofty prices had not yet been "raped." Avon's 1974 price plunge would demonstrate shortly the precariousness of that virginity.

My distrust of establishment advice deepened during 1974 as a result of another investment misadventure that turned out to be a good deal more painful than the Citibank affair. Another establishment bank was indirectly involved.

The story really begins all the way back in September of 1967. But let me start at a later point, on a bright June morning in 1974. I arrived early in the newspaper's Cortlandt Street office, a few blocks north of Wall Street, on that particular morning. With a busy schedule ahead, I turned quickly to the pile of new mail on my desk. As usual, it was forbiddingly fat and, again as usual, it was made up to a discouraging degree of useless press releases, predestined for my wastebasket. But sandwiched among them was something very special—a note from a *Wall Street Journal* colleague named Dave McClintick. Dave was one of our very finest investigative reporters, with a talent that I suspect had no relationship to the fact that he also was a Harvard graduate and an avid fan of Frank Sinatra. The note, which Dave had apparently typed the previous evening and then deposited on my desk, read as follows:

Al,

I'm doing a story on Home-Stake Production Company. Couldn't help noticing on the participants' list that you're an investor. Story is finished and skedded to run soon. I've held off mentioning to you because I didn't want any outside adversary ever to be able to make a case that we were motivated to do the story because a WSJ editor was an investor. I didn't get the investor list until well into the reporting. Needless to say, the story doesn't mention you.

No one else in the office knows you're on the list, with one exception. I asked Dick Rustin to look at it for brokers' names and forgot to delete yours. He spotted it, but swears he'll keep mum. He's certainly one of the most discreet people in the office.

Be happy to discuss the story with you anytime, or leave it be, as you desire.

Rgds,
Dave McClintick

I opted not to discuss my involvement in the dismal Home-Stake matter partly out of embarrassment: An editor of the country's leading financial publication turns out to be a naïve participant in what the paper calls the biggest investment swindle of the decade. Who would want to read the advice—on the economy, on investment strategy, on anything—of such a dupe? A larger consideration was my conviction that Dave McClintick might well walk off at the end of the year with a Pulitzer Prize for his sleuthing of the Home-Stake mess. Disclosing my involvement, I feared, might hurt his chances. (He did not, although his piece about the collapsing oil-drilling concern did earn him the paper's nomination for a Pulitzer and, I understand, his entry came close to winning the coveted award.)

My ignorance of Dave's project, I should add, was not as extraordinary as it may sound. My bailiwick of business and finance was far removed from the paper's investigatory endeavors. As at other publications, our investigative reporters tended, then as now, to be a special breed, often working quietly and alone for weeks at a stretch on a single story, with perhaps only one or two editors even cognizant of the particular project. Accordingly, Dave's weeks of probing into the tangled affairs of my Home-Stake investment were utterly unknown to me, and his hastily typed note that morning came as a total surprise.

The story of Home-Stake was later spelled out by Dave in a 335-page book titled *Stealing from the Rich: The Home-Stake Oil Swindle*, published in 1977 by M. Evans & Co. The details of how a small group of Oklahoma-based promoters managed to get scores of supposedly sophisticated people to sink money into a series of ill-fated oil-drilling programs makes fascinating reading. The list of big-name entertainers who put money into the venture between 1967 and 1974 included such people as Jack Benny, Tony Curtis, Faye Dunaway, Mia Farrow, Walter Matthau, Barbra Streisand, Barbara Walters, and Jonathan Winters. But far more startling, at least to me, is the list of supposedly astute business people who also sank many thousands into Home-Stake. If ever there was evidence that the nation's business establishment could invest unwisely, that list is it. Here are some of the names, along with business posts held before, while, or after the Home-Stake investments were made:

Hoyt Ammidon, chairman of the United States Trust Co.; Lewis W. Foy, president of Bethlehem Steel Corp.; Thomas S.

Gates, Jr., chairman of Morgan Guaranty Trust Co.; Donald M. Kendall, chairman of PepsiCo Inc.; David J. Mahoney, Jr., chairman of Norton Simon Inc.; Neil H. McElroy, chairman of Procter & Gamble Co.; Russell W. McFall, chairman of Western Union Corp.; Ernest L. Molloy, president of R. H. Macy & Co.; George S. Moore, chairman of Citicorp; Chester W. Nimitz, Jr., chairman of Perkin-Elmer Corp.; Robert S. Oelman, chairman of NCR Corp.; James R. Shepley, president of Time Inc.; Muriel Siebert, first female member of the New York Stock Exchange; Donald B. Smiley, chairman of R. H. Macy & Co.; William I. Spencer, president of Citicorp; J. Howard Wood, chairman, executive committee, Chicago Tribune Co.; Walter B. Wriston, chairman of Citicorp; Fred J. Borch, chairman of General Electric Co.; Robert B. Fiske, Jr., a former U.S. Attorney and a partner of the law firm of Davis, Polk & Wardwell; George N. Lindsay, a partner of the law firm of Debevoise, Plimpton, Lyons & Gates, and brother of John V. Lindsay, former mayor of New York City; and William A. Shea, a New York lawyer for whom Shea Stadium is named.

Without a doubt, I had blundered into distinguished company. And my being there was a consequence of my own naïve confidence back in 1967 that an investment looking good to leaders of the establishment, an investment in which the establishment itself was risking money, was bona fide, good for me, the proverbial little guy.

My involvement began when a neighbor, a stockbroker with a now-defunct New York securities firm, began urging me to put a bit of money into Home-Stake Production Co., a Tulsa-based concern with drilling operations in oil and gas and not to be confused with the similarly named gold-mining concern. Home-Stake Production had been offering participating interests to investors for some ten years and, according to my broker friend, promised not only considerable tax advantages, as a highly deductible drilling operation, but also a real prospect of healthy, rising earnings in the years to come. My friend stressed that its focus—on achieving a so-called secondary, or steam-induced, recovery of oil already known to be in the vicinity—

entailed far less risk than most drilling programs designed as tax shelters.

A timid soul, and one whose income hardly justified extensive concern about the tax bite, I hesitated. My years on Wall Street had already taught me to be highly skeptical of all "surefire" investments, especially any that revolved around a tax-shelter inducement. My broker friend persisted. I hesitated. But then my friend told me that among the enthusiastic investors in Home-Stake was none other than the chairman of the board of the United States Trust Co. of New York, the aforementioned Mr. Ammidon. The U. S. Trust Co. wasn't simply an old and famous Wall Street institution with a lineage dating back some two hundred years. It was also the manager of my profit-sharing and retirement program, the nest egg that I had been struggling to build up for the days when my newspaper career would be over. Indeed, I was aware that U. S. Trust had been managing the *Journal*'s employee retirement program since the plan's inception soon after World War II.

Hoyt Ammidon, for me, was the clincher. If Home-Stake was good enough for that august banker, the guardian of my retirement money, it surely was good enough for me. If further persuasion by my broker friend was required for me to plunk down my money for a stake in Home-Stake, it was my friend's report that such other luminaries as Fred J. Borch of General Electric were also prominent Home-Stake investors.

And so, in December of 1967, I enthusiastically became a participant in an oil-drilling operation that seven years later was very nearly to win Dave McClintick the Pulitzer Prize for investigative reporting.

Through a considerable portion of those seven years, I remained blissfully unaware of just how sour an investment I had made. The eventual bonanza in earnings that my broker friend had talked glowingly about back in 1967 did not materialize. But the company's reports, spewing regularly from Tulsa, seemed increasingly optimistic, to the extent that I was able to decipher the petroleum industry jargon.

In fact, as Dave McClintick eventually reported, the company all the while was slowly sliding into bankruptcy, under circumstances that would lead to charges against some of the Home-Stake management, in 1973, that its drilling operations had been vastly overstated. Among the charges were conspiracy and mail fraud. The president of the outfit, after a drawn-out series of legislative delays, was fined $19,000, the maximum allowed for the ten felony crimes of which he stood convicted. He was also ordered to pay $100,000 to the Home-Stake bankruptcy referee for, according to the judge in the case, "the benefit of widows, orphans or children of participants or destitute participants. . . ."

Not widowed nor an orphan, I placed no claim for a share of that $100,000. My Home-Stake investment, fortunately far smaller than those held by most of my prominent coparticipants, had become virtually valueless. I felt angry that the court hadn't come down harder on the company's managers. I admired Dave McClintick's reporting skill in unraveling the mess, and his discretion. And, most importantly, I learned the hazards of placing one's faith in the perspicacity of supposedly astute leaders of the establishment. Citibank's devotion to Avon had been an eye-opener. The devotion to Home-Stake of a whole galaxy of establishment leaders drove home the harsh lesson:

Don't make an investment simply because someone with impressive credentials recommends, plans to make, or previously has made a similar investment.

4.
Mavericks

BE YOUR OWN INVESTMENT MANAGER. BE WARY OF THE ESTABlishment, the famous financial institutions, the giant, welladvertised banks and brokerage houses who would oversee your nest egg and safely shepherd your savings in a perilous economic climate.

The message—to be wary—seems unmistakable. And there's an additional dimension to this distrust that warrants attention for the light it sheds on why the investment advice of big-name institutions is so often so bad. It can best be sketched, perhaps, by telling about a few individuals whose faces have never appeared on the cover of, say, *Time* magazine—people like John Exter and A. Gary Shilling and William Tehan.

What do these relatively obscure people have in common?

Four things: (1) Each once worked for a large institution within the financial establishment. (2) Each espoused views about the business outlook that conflicted with the conventional wisdom of the time. (3) Each gave up jobs within the establishment. (4) Each was eventually proved largely correct in his view of the economic outlook.

John Exter

Let's consider first the tribulations, and eventual triumphs, of John Exter.

Rare is the economic forecaster who runs against the herd. Rarer still is the economic forecaster who runs against the herd and also works for an organization that possesses real clout in the financial world—a major bank or corporation or brokerage house. To be such a maverick takes some courage—you could embarrass your employer or even lose your job.

A striking specimen of this rare breed of forecaster is John Exter. In 1972 Mr. Exter was a senior vice president of one of the most prestigious financial organizations in the world, our old friend Citibank. For thirteen years Mr. Exter, whose pre-Citibank background included a string of important Federal Reserve posts, had been speaking his mind on economic matters. For thirteen years his superiors and colleagues at the institution had tolerated, with growing reluctance, his extraordinary candor.

That was a time, even more than nowadays, when all too many economists were under pressure from their bosses to see, hear, and speak no evil about business or—particularly—stockmarket prospects. Citibank's reluctance to muzzle Mr. Exter, by comparison with attitudes elsewhere, seemed downright refreshing. And the bank's hierarchy certainly must have felt the temptation to apply a muzzle. For few forecasters on Wall Street or Main Street had been so steadfastly concerned in 1972 about prospects for international monetary stability and the eventual impact of any instability on business in general, including the stock market. (If only John Exter had been managing that portfolio of ours that summer in London, instead of the more conventional gentlemen, his colleagues, who fancied Avon Products!)

An interview with John Exter, conducted in March of 1972, shows the man's extraordinary ability to take an independent—and as things turned out, remarkably prescient—line on the outlook:

—As to the stock market, although he stressed that he would

never attempt to forecast precise price trends, he said that his basic concern about international monetary matters led him to be wary about stock prices in coming months. The one major exception: gold-mining shares, which traditionally have shown strength during periods of monetary disorder.

—As to the economy in general, the senior vice president envisaged a worsening liquidity squeeze, to be characterized by increasing pressure on various types of debtors, individuals, and corporations. He boldly predicted—and was soon proved correct—that a recent realignment of international currency exchange rates would "rip apart at the seams any day now." This was hardly, I should note, the standard gospel preached by the top officers of Citibank at that time.

Mr. Exter's reasoning is worth recalling. "Debt has been created at an excessive rate," he warned, "not only in the United States but throughout much of the industrial world." Viewing the U.S. situation, he cautioned that the Federal Reserve "is locked into a credit squeeze that dares not stop, a prisoner of its own expansionism; if it were to stop, or even try seriously to decelerate, interest rates would rise sharply and many debtors would have problems."

Remember, the time was early 1972, a period of brisk economic growth and relatively little inflation, well before the years of double-digit interest rates and soaring business failures.

The Exter scenario went on. "At some point," he said, "no matter how expansionist the Federal Reserve may be, interest rates will rise anyway." And, he continued, "as rates generally climb, economic growth will slow and a new, more intensified liquidity squeeze than those experienced in recent years will develop." It would be an understatement to say that most of Mr. Exter's colleagues at Citibank—or at any of the other top dozen or so banks around the nation—professed a far more sanguine view of the stock market and the economy as a whole. In fact, later in 1972 the gulf between Mr. Exter and his Citibank colleagues became so great that, cut off from mainstream thinking at the bank, he decided in May to accept, at age sixty-one, early retirement.

For years, the banker recalls, his influence within the institution's policy-making circles had been eroding. His conviction that severe inflation, soaring interest rates, and mind-boggling gold prices lay ahead began to take hold as long ago as 1962. At that time, putting his money where his mouth happened to be, he made the first of many remarkable personal investment decisions. He sharply increased the mortgage on his New Jersey home, borrowing at a rate of 5¼ percent, and then plowed the proceeds of the loan into shares of gold-mining stocks, whose prices and dividend payments subsequently soared more sharply than even the cost of the New Jersey real estate.

In 1964 John Exter was still influential enough, as a senior vice president at the bank, to hold a seat on a committee there that helped decide such key concerns as the makeup of the bank's securities portfolio. In 1964, Mr. Exter recalls, he urged Citibank to begin selling off its considerable municipal-bond holdings, as a precaution against the time, which he foresaw, when inflation and spiraling interest rates would depress the value of such securities. "I was overruled and, in fact, regarded as something of a nut for even suggesting such an idea," he says.

Mr. Exter's clout continued to wane at Citibank. While he continued to receive periodic pay increases, he feels strongly that "my compensation was held down in the latter years." By the spring of 1972 he found himself sequestered in a large office, still with a secretary, but with nothing much to do. His supposed responsibility was to keep top management abreast of international monetary developments. In fact, his counsel was seldom sought and even less frequently heeded. Worse, when he would occasionally speak out publicly he felt a pressure to tone down his gloomy views about the outlook. In brief, although he was first and foremost an economist, at Harvard with Nobel laureate Paul Samuelson, and extensively trained within the Federal Reserve system, he was hesitant to speak his mind about the economy.

One time he did, at a meeting of wealthy investors in Hamilton, Bermuda, in 1971. A *Wall Street Journal* reporter happened to be in the audience. The gloomy Exter speech was duly reported in the newspaper and, subsequently, read within Citibank executive offices. "I caught a lot of static over that," Mr. Exter recalls. "It was the last time, until leaving the bank, that I really spoke my mind in public." The advice dispensed in that speech, for the record, would have yielded huge investment profits—largely in gold-mining stock—for anyone who followed it. Among the securities decidedly *not* on Mr. Exter's recommended list in Bermuda was Avon Products.

After leaving Citibank in May of 1972, Mr. Exter proceeded to set up his own business as a private economic consultant and investment counselor, working from his home in Mountain Lakes, New Jersey. There, he makes himself available to anyone, bull or bear, willing to pay for his advice. His clients range from wealthy individuals to the pension fund for state employees of Alaska. His yearly earnings from such clients and from lecture engagements amount to approximately triple what he reckons he would be netting were he still at Citibank.

A. Gary Shilling

The brief encounter that A. Gary Shilling had with the country's investment establishment in some ways is even more disturbing than John Exter's experience at Citibank. John Exter's counsel was disregarded within the bank's ruling circles. If his superiors there chose not to heed him, that was their prerogative, for better or worse.

Gary Shilling's employer in the late 1960s was Merrill Lynch, Pierce, Fenner & Smith, now simply Merrill Lynch & Co., the largest financial-services concern in the Wall Street area or, for that matter, in the nation. Mr. Shilling's wisdom was a marketable commodity for his employer, like John Exter's. As Merrill Lynch's chief economist, he was an important front man for the firm. He was expected to make speeches, to issue frequent appraisals of the economic outlook, and, generally, to get his name and the firm's name into magazines and newspapers. He would discover, however, that there were limits to his employer's hunger for publicity.

I first met Mr. Shilling in the late 1960s, when he was new at Merrill Lynch. He was, I recall, only twenty-nine years old, a remarkable age for a man serving as chief economist at such a large firm. His work had attracted my attention when he correctly predicted, almost to the day, a generally unanticipated devaluation of the British pound. This was quite an accomplishment at a time when most currency exchange rates were fixed in relation to one another and a devaluation of any major currency represented big financial news.

By late in 1969 I had grown to respect Mr. Shilling's ability to forecast economic developments. Accordingly, I was duly impressed when he called me a day or two before Christmas to report that he looked for a major recession just down the road. At the time, this was a gloomier view than that put forward by most forecasters. The majority opinion was that no recession loomed. Most economists simply felt that business would slow down for a while and then resume moving along a path of continuing economic expansion. My friend at Merrill Lynch, as things tunred out, proved eminently right. A full-scale recession did indeed start in late 1969, and it lasted, getting persistently deeper, for some twelve months. Mr. Shilling's forecast of all this appeared under my by-line on December 26, 1969. The headline on the article read: "MERRILL LYNCH CHIEF ECONOMIST SEES BUSINESS HEADED INTO MAJOR RECESSION."

Donald T. Regan, Secretary of the Treasury in the Reagan administration, who headed Merrill Lynch at that time, was immediately upset to discover that his chief economist had publicly forecast a major recession, an eventuality hardly likely to spur stock-purchasing. He proceeded to let Mr. Shilling know about his displeasure in blunt terms. Mr. Shilling recalls, among other things, that his bonus—an important part of his yearly compensation in those days—was cut sharply a short time after his recession forecast appeared. In the following weeks, as the recession deepened, I observed that Mr. Shilling's forecasts became less and less frequent in Merrill Lynch press releases and, when they occasionally did surface, they seemed blander and more cautious.

Later, Mr. Shilling was relieved of his responsibilities as the firm's chief economist and assigned to duty merely as one of several economists working not for the parent company but for a recently acquired investment-advisory subsidiary. Later still, Mr. Shilling decided to quit his Merrill Lynch employment and seek other, more challenging work. He later became chief economist for White, Weld & Co., another large Wall Street securities firm. However, when that firm became financially troubled during the late 1970s Mr. Shilling quit that job as well. A major factor in his decision was that Merrill Lynch, his old employer, had moved to acquire the business of White, Weld.

Mr. Shilling at this time decided to strike out on his own. He established a small economics consulting service that bears his name. In recent years, his firm has acquired a growing list of individual and corporate customers.

In short, he emerged successfully from a difficult period within the confines of the establishment. One lesson that clearly comes from his tribulations is, once again, that investors should be wary of the advice dished out publicly by big-name institutions. Be aware that forecasters employed by such institutions can easily antagonize their superiors if they sound too pessimistic about the business outlook—at least in public. Many establishment executives seem to believe that gloomy forecasts can actually create a gloomy economy. By and large, their profits are fattest when business generally is expanding. Mr. Shilling's experience at Merrill Lynch, if nothing else, makes clear the importance of attempting to see the economic picture for yourself, not depending on what establishment economists may be saying.

A happy ending, quite obviously, has followed the escapes—I believe that is the appropriate word—of both John Exter and Gary Shilling from muzzling jobs. An even happier ending belongs to William Tehan, whose experiences within the establishment were even more trying than those of Messrs. Exter and Shilling.

William Tehan

William Tehan was graduated from Amherst College in 1955 and from there went to work for Citibank. He worked there from 1955 to 1958. In 1958 he married and landed a job with his wife's father, the head of a family plastics-producing company in Worcester, Massachusetts. Mr. Tehan worked as a production manager, supervising the molding of plastics for television screens, vacuum-cleaner nozzles, radio cabinets, television cabinets, flashlights, and other industrial and consumer products. In 1960 he decided to leave the world of plastics and try his hand on Wall Street. He wanted a position as a research analyst, and he had a keen desire to learn the fundamentals of investing. After about eight months, he obtained a job in the research department of Hayden, Stone & Co., a well-known brokerage house in New York. He did research for its oil analyst and its mining and metals analyst for about a year and then became assistant to the mining and metals analyst. About two years later he was promoted to senior mining and metals analyst. During this time, he took night courses at New York University in accounting and securities analysis.

While Mr. Tehan worked in the research department of Hayden, Stone, in early 1962, the stock market suffered a sharp break. "All of the securities which I had recommended in my capacity as an analyst went down substantially," he recalls, "and this was quite a shock and eye-opener to me. I had talked with all of the companies which I had recommended and had good earnings projections from each of them. This experience of declining securities prices in the face of good earnings prospects made me realize that there must be external forces outside of the corporate structure which influenced the outlook for earnings and therefore stock prices."

Mr. Tehan continues: "With this thought in mind, I embarked upon a study of the business cycle in the United States, starting with the Civil War, to develop some knowledge of what were the basic influences on securities prices, and on the business outlook itself. Between 1962 and 1965, I think I read every book available on the history of the business cycle, the various booms and busts, and on interest rates and on gold."

In 1964 Mr. Tehan left Hayden, Stone and went to work for Dominick & Dominick Inc., another well-known Wall Street house. He was hired initially to work in the institutional sales department. In 1965, he recalls, he began to feel that an "easy-money policy" of the Federal Reserve in Washington was leading to a situation in which America's balance-of-payments deficit would grow immensely. He was convinced, as a consequence, that interest rates would rise. Like Gary Schilling, William Tehan also was sure that the British pound was headed for a devaluation.

Altogether, he saw a situation developing that threatened the stability of the then-prevailing international monetary system of fixed currency exchange rates, known as the Bretton Woods system, after the New Hampshire town where planners met in 1944 to establish the arrangement. However, having adopted what he calls this "bearish viewpoint," Mr. Tehan found that he could not sell it to Dominick's institutional clients. Discouraged, he transferred to the firm's retail sales department, where he felt he would have a better chance of convincing individual customers of his gloomy views on the outlook for interest rates, the dollar, the economy, and the stock market.

About this time, Dominick, which had been a one-office firm since its founding in the nineteenth century, began to embark on an expansion program. This was launched by younger partners who had in recent years been appointed by Gardner and Varick Stout, senior partners approaching retirement age. The younger partners wanted to expand the business of the firm in a drive to increase its earnings.

In 1965 Mr. Tehan began to move his retail-client accounts out of the stock market, particularly out of such blue-chip stocks as General Motors, Du Pont, and American Telephone & Telegraph. When interest rates began to rise during that summer, Mr. Tehan went in to see Gardner Stout to explain why he was so bearish about the general outlook.

"I suggested to him that perhaps the firm should reconsider its expansion program because if the liquidity squeeze which I saw coming actually developed, Dominick would be in serious financial trouble," Mr. Tehan recalls. "Gardner replied that he thought I was entirely wrong and that 'no bears live on Fifth Avenue.' With the expansion of Dominick under way, interest rates rose and the stock and bond markets suffered serious declines in 1966. Later, of course, these markets headed into a sustained period of turbulence."

Let Mr. Tehan continue his story:

"In the fall of 1965, the sales manager of Dominick & Dominick pointed out to me that the firm had never done any business with the Amherst College Endowment Fund, which was then worth about $100,000,000. I knew the treasurer of the college quite well, and the sales manager of the firm asked me if I would call on him to see if we could develop a business relationship. The treasurer of Amherst at that time was Stanley Teele, a retired dean of the Harvard Business School, who had come to Amherst shortly before to be treasurer. When I made my first visit to see Dr. Teele, he asked me what I wanted to sell him. I told him I wanted to sell him on the idea of taking the Amherst portfolio out of common stock. This concept interested him and I explained why I thought it was something that should be done. I gave him my views about the expansive, inflationary posture of the Federal Reserve, the prospect of persistently rising interest rates, and the deterioration I expected in the U.S. balance of payments.

"Dr. Teele and I embarked on a program to sell a substantial proportion of Amherst College's common stocks, particularly General Motors and Du Pont, which we sold near their all-time highs in 1965. Dr. Teele pointed out to me, however, that in order to complete a major liquidation of common stocks he would need some kind of written analysis to present to his finance committee, in order to win them over and give some basic reason for his posture. He asked if I would write an analysis of the balance-of-payments and interest-rate problems to present to the Amherst Board of Trustees at their scheduled meeting. I presented this written analysis in about two weeks to Dr. Teele. He said he was impressed and had copies made for each of the trustees. Of course, I did this on my own, for Dr. Teele and the trustees of Amherst, without informing anyone at Dominick.

"In the spring of 1966, one of the trustees of Amherst, Eustace Seligman, a senior partner of Sullivan & Cromwell, the big New York law firm, was returning from the Bahamas on an airplane with Varick Stout. Seligman commented to Stout in the course of their conversation that he was impressed with the study which Dominick had done on the U.S. dollar problem. Varick said that he was not aware of such a study and, upon that comment, Seligman pulled from his briefcase a copy of the dollar study which I had given to Stanley Teele for the Amherst trustees. Varick read it over and on his return to Dominick from his vacation he suggested to the sales manager that this study should be published for Dominick's overseas clients. But the sales manager was entirely opposed and very annoyed to say the least at my having written the paper. It did not, to put it mildly, enhance my career prospects at the firm."

In 1966 a client of Mr. Tehan's registered a complaint with the firm, claiming that he had managed the client's account in such a way as to lose the client some money. The firm investigated the assertion and, although Dominick's in-house lawyer reported to the partners that his investigation showed no impropriety, the aforementioned sales manager took this opportunity, as Mr. Tehan puts it, to "have me fired." This occurred in October of 1967.

A footnote: The interest-rate spiral and concurrent liquidity squeeze of 1969–70 hit Dominick, as well as other Wall Street houses, hard.

Meanwhile, Mr. Tehan managed to find a job with White, Weld & Co., the Wall Street house that also once employed Gary Shilling. It's now a part of Merrill Lynch. He worked in its Park Avenue office, where the manager, he recalls, "was aware of my bearish posture and my recent investment interest in gold-mining shares as solid investments for the stormy economic weather that I saw ahead." The manager warned him, Mr. Tehan recalls, that it would be necessary for him to tone down his bearishness, pay attention to White, Weld's far less gloomy research findings, and "do more in common-stock buying other than just gold-mining shares; I was, of course, desperate for a job at that time and indicated to him that I would consider this request."

Mr. Tehan had been at White, Weld about two weeks when the Bank of England devalued the pound, a move that triggered the greatest investment rush into gold shares known in America up to that time. "I was flooded with requests to purchase gold-mining shares for existing and many new accounts," the broker recounts. This situation created a problem at White, Weld, Mr. Tehan claims, because "many partners of the firm and its research department did not understand nor believe in gold-mining investments. Just as I had at Dominick, I tried to explain to some of the partners who questioned me about my view on interest rates and gold that the country was in a liquidity squeeze which would get more intense as time went on."

The research department did not agree. Worse, it rankled that Mr. Tehan persisted in disregarding its more conventional investment recommendations. "The situation became as abrasive at White, Weld as it had been at Dominick," he says.

Mr. Tehan left White, Weld in December of 1969. During the next three months, he went throughout the Wall Street financial community seeking a job where he would be able freely to put into practice his bearish convictions about the economic outlook. "I couldn't find a firm at all interested," he remembers, until "in March of 1970 I met Phil Herzig of P. R. Herzig & Co., a very small nonestablishment securities firm, at a cocktail party. In the course of our discussion, I asked him how he ran a brokerage firm profitably and still took proper care of his clients. He replied to me that he bought gold-mining shares, because he felt this was the only true long-term investment which would make money for clients and at the same time keep the firm alive." The two men had lunch the next day and agreed that Mr. Tehan would be taken on for one year at a salary of $18,000.

"My original effort at P. R. Herzig," Mr. Tehan recalls, "was to explain to institutions why they should move capital out of conventional stocks and bonds and into gold-mining shares to weather the storms ahead. Phil Herzig and I spent six months talking to banks, mutual funds, and other such outfits, but could not make any real headway. Accordingly, after six or seven months, we abandoned the effort to attract institutional customers and shifted our energies toward the development of a retail business, focusing on individual accounts, trying to explain to people why major changes should be made in investment portfolios, changes which should include a significant commitment to gold and gold-mining shares."

Of course, such a strategy worked out to be tremendously successful during the torrid inflation that subsequently developed in the United States and elsewhere. Mr. Tehan recounts one happy experience: "In 1971 a wealthy Midwestern manufacturer came to New York to seek the advice of a prominent Wall Street investment adviser. This Midwesterner had made a fortune in manufacturing and was interested in having professional management to protect his assets. In the course of their discussion, this wealthy man made one specification—that at least 15 percent or 20 percent of his funds be invested in gold-mining shares. The famous investment adviser said he did not agree with the idea and did not know anything about gold-mining shares. But he did say that he knew of a man, Bill Tehan, who was recommending gold-mining shares, and he added, 'That dumb sonofabitch is ruining his reputation by doing so.'"

The manufacturer came to see Mr. Tehan at P. R. Herzig. "I explained to him," the broker recalls, "our investment view and how we felt about gold-mining shares. This man and his family became very good clients, and in 1971 we began to invest their funds in gold-mining shares. On the day that gold first crossed the $100-per-ounce mark—I think it was in 1973—I received a telegram from the man which read as follows: 'Congratulations to the dumbest sonofabitch I know.' "

5.
Nowhere to Turn

MESSRS. TEHAN, SHILLING, AND EXTER, ESTABLISHMENT REJECTS all, would have been prime fellows to have listened to for investment advice in the 1960s and early 1970s. By and large, their counsel would have enriched investors during a treacherous time. For example, in an interview at the start of 1973, William Tehan offered this advice: "I would get completely out of the stock market. I would put one third of my money in gold-mining shares and the rest in currency or in U.S. Treasury bills."

When the statement was made, the Dow Jones industrial stock average was slightly above the 1000 mark. It had been gradually rising for about six months, and much of the advice emanating from establishment firms along Wall Street at that time was unabashedly optimistic: Stay with the blue-chip, big-name stocks; the stock market will move much higher in coming months with the Dow Jones average crossing 1500.

Let's briefly review the actual performance of the Dow Jones average in the months just after Mr. Tehan's warning. By May 1973, less than five months later, it was below 900. By September of the same year it was under 800. Late the following summer, the stock average dropped below 700. In the fall of 1974 it plunged down through the 600 level. In December of 1974, less than two years after Mr. Tehan's warning to get out of the stock market, the Dow Jones average stood at 577.60, down from a high of 1051.70 in January of 1973, when the warning was sounded. That works out to a decline in stock prices of about 45 percent.

A part of Mr. Tehan's investment advice at the start of 1973 was to invest heavily in gold-mining shares. The average price of such shares is tracked regularly by *Barron's*, the weekly business magazine. In early 1973, when Mr. Tehan gave his warning, *Barron's* group average for gold stocks stood at about 150. A year later the same average was at 400. And by mid-1974, with the Dow Jones average skidding toward its December nadir of 577.60, the gold-mining group touched the 600 mark.

A footnote: When Mr. Tehan urged an investment in gold-mining stocks, the price of the yellow metal was about $90 an ounce. In the 1973 interview, he predicted that this price would rise within the decade to "the area of $500 to $1,000 an ounce," which, of course, is precisely what happened. In 1979 gold crossed $800 an ounce, a level that even surprised most "goldbugs"—as chrysophiles are labeled by their more conventional colleagues within the investment community. The attitude of the Wall Street establishment toward gold investments in early 1973 can be indicated, perhaps, by recalling a conversation that I had with an officer of the Bank of New York, an old-line institution, not unlike Mr. Ammidon's U. S. Trust. The Bank of New York also happened by then to be the guardian of *The Wall Street Journal's* profit-sharing program, the account having been shifted from U. S. Trust.

I was lunching with this Bank of New York officer in the Wall Street area. Aware that one of my companion's responsibilities at the Bank of New York was managing the mixture of securities in the newspaper's profit-sharing portfolio, I also knew that he, like me, felt uneasy about the general economic outlook—including prospects for many of the blue-chip securities contained in our profit-sharing program's portfolio. I further knew that he, like me, suspected that the months ahead might be a time for what Wall Streeters in their jargon call "a defensive investment stance." Knowing that gold-mining stocks were traditionally regarded as rainy-day investments, if highly volatile, I asked the banker why in the world the newspaper's portfolio contained no such issues and, in fact, was so heavily invested in the more conventional sort of stocks that would surely tend to depreciate if the economy turned sour, as we both anticipated would happen in the months ahead.

His reply: "Gold shares are simply not the sort of thing that the bank believes in. If we were to move to place such securities in your profit-sharing portfolio, I can assure you that I'd be quickly overruled. It's the sort of investment one can readily undertake for a personal portfolio, but not on an institutional basis when one is supposedly acting with great professional prudence to safeguard the retirement money of others. Bank policy deems such stocks highly speculative."

Years later, in 1980, a brilliant and unusually articulate economist, Albert M. Wojnilower of First Boston Corp. in New York, looked back over the sorry investment performance of most Wall Street money managers during the preceding decade. His conclusion: "In truth, the speculator has become the prudent man today. Many of the pension fund managers and other fiduciaries whom we have charged to be the prudent guardians of our assets have learned the dangerous lesson that they must now be speculators."

Surely, back in 1973 the wise gray heads at the Bank of New York who managed the money in *The Wall Street Journal*'s retirement program would have deemed themselves rank speculators and most imprudent had they taken those nest-egg funds of ours out of the familiar famous-name securities—IBM, General Electric, and the rest—and placed them into the unfamiliar and tongue-twisting issues suggested by the likes of William Tehan—gold-mining issues like Hartebeestfontein and West Driefontein and Blyvooruitzicht.

Who would have dreamt that the stock of such companies

would fare far better in the coming months and years, would prove a far more "prudent" investment, than the traditional blue-chip corporations so greatly admired and heavily bought by the country's most prestigious investment advisers?

Credentials

William Tehan's prescient advice represents an extreme illustration of an ironic situation—the establishment outcast being entirely right about the investment future and the famous names being wrong. The same can be said of men like John Exter and Gary Shilling. But a few words should also be inserted about credentials. It so happens that Messrs. Tehan, Shilling, and Exter are all graduates of eminent institutions— respectively, Amherst, Stanford, and Harvard. This may be coincidental, for the plain truth is that impressive credentials and an impressive record of investment advice don't necessarily go together. Don't suppose that because a man has many degrees his management of money will prove more astute than that of the fellow with no degrees.

The point was driven home to me in 1973, the year that Mr. Tehan was urging investors to get out of blue-chip stocks and into gold-mining stocks. I recall the case of two exceedingly disparate forecasters, one laden with academic credentials and working for a top Wall Street brokerage house, the other lacking credentials and self-employed. The two were Robert H. Parks, who served in 1973 as the number-one economist of Blyth Eastman Dillon & Co., a well-known New York securities company, and Harry D. Schultz, the publisher of an economic newsletter with several thousand loyal subscribers.

Dr. Parks, to say the least, possessed impressive credentials. The "Dr." that he used before his name was well earned. He had received a bachelor's degree from Swarthmore, a master's and a doctorate from the University of Pennsylvania, and had held professorships at two universities.

Harry Schultz once told a *Wall Street Journal* reporter that the "Dr." he used before his name reflected a degree received from St. Lawrence University in New York State. But the name of Harry D. Schultz, it turned out upon investigation, was utterly unknown to officials at that institution. "We find no indication that one Mr. Harry Schultz ever attended St. Lawrence University at any time, or that he ever received an honorary degree from this university," declared an officer of the Canton, New York, institution. It does appear that Harry Schultz did spend about two years at City College of Los Angeles, where he majored not in economics or finance but in journalism.

The question is: Which man's view of the economic future would you tend to put your faith in—that of Dr. Parks or that of "Dr." Schultz?

In mid-1973, if you had taken the counsel of Robert Parks, you would no doubt have kept much of your money invested in the U.S. stock market in blue-chip companies—and you would have lost a great deal of money. Harry Schultz, on the other hand, was urging his newsletter subscribers to invest in South African gold-mining stocks which, as we have seen, subsequently appreciated enormously. Around the time that Harry Schultz was recommending such stocks to his subscribers, Dr. Parks told Blyth Eastman clients, in a special report, that: "King Gold is dead." As noted earlier, the price of gold in early 1973 was $90 an ounce.

The lesson once again is clear: Be your own investment counselor and don't be awed by advisers who have imposing credentials.

It should be stressed, of course, that Robert Parks was by no means alone in his gloomy appraisal of gold's future. Indeed, his view of gold's prospects typified what was echoed by no less a Wall Street figure, for example, than Robert Roosa, an eminent member of the financial establishment, a partner of Brown Brothers Harriman, an old-line private bank in the Wall Street area. Earlier, Mr. Roosa served in Washington as a top official of the Treasury Department and earlier still as an official within the Federal Reserve System. Around the time that Harry

Schultz was urging gold purchases for investors, Mr. Roosa was predicting that the per-ounce price of the yellow metal might drop to as low as $6.00.

Men like Harry Schultz were "among the first to appreciate the significance of the continuing international payments deficits of this country, as well as the flood of U.S. dollars overseas," states a retrospective study issued in 1980 by Argus Research Corp., a New York investment research concern. The study continues: "Moreover, they correctly perceived gold and gold-mining equities as an insurance policy that would enable investors to shield their wealth from the decline in our money's purchasing power." Harry Schultz "recognized before Wall Street that government policies of the last two-to-four decades must lead to an erosion of the dollar's value and, therefore, investors would require new routes to preserve capital," says Charles Grayson, a public relations executive in Princeton, New Jersey, who has known and conducted business with Harry Schultz over many years.

An editorial appearing in *Fortune* magazine in the spring of 1980 also acknowledges the prescience of various nonestablishment individuals who constitute "what Wall Street continues to regard as the lunatic fringe." These people—men like Harry Schultz and William Tehan—"have done better by their customers than those plausible fellows who keep putting us into stocks and bonds" regardless of the economic situation, the editorial states. It concludes: "We don't claim they're sane—only that, under some presidents, their advice has been profitable."

Executive Insight

It should come as no surprise that top business executives—the highly paid chieftains of giant corporations, the clients of Wall Street's financial establishment—generally exhibit only a minimal degree of insight into the economic outlook. In mid-April of 1980, precisely when the U.S. economy was nosediving in the seventh bona fide recession of the post-World War II era, the following report was issued by Dun & Bradstreet Corp.:

"Business optimism has perked up considerably from the sag begun midway in 1979. . . . Among the 1,499 executives interviewed about prospects for 1980's second quarter, strengthening confidence was noted in regard to sales, new orders and profits. . . . More of the executives, particularly in retailing, anticipated additions to their payrolls, and fewer, notably in durable-goods manufacturing, anticipated a cut in rosters."

As we know now, unemployment was soaring—particularly in durable-goods industries—at the very time that survey was being taken. A general economic recession had begun back in January and was continuing to deepen.

Around the same time, a similar survey taken by New York's nonprofit Conference Board found that the "business confidence of more than 1,600 chief executives around the country rose in the first quarter of 1980."

It's noteworthy that this rising confidence in a nosediving economy was not generally shared by the typical American consumer. Another Conference Board survey, taken about the same time, found that "the confidence of American consumers in the U.S. economy fell for the fourth consecutive month." The survey, which covers over five thousand households across the country, has repeatedly proved a far more accurate measure of the economy's general course, according to a Conference Board official, than other surveys focusing just on the view from the executive suite.

An analysis by Manufacturers Hanover Trust in New York attempts to explore reasons for this "incredible dichotomy of views." The conclusion:

"It is possible that executives have been misled by the profits picture in the first quarter; calculations made by this bank, based on the Commerce Department's first-quarter gross national product figures, suggest that pretax earnings jumped 14% in the first quarter of 1980, compared with the same period a year earlier. This is about twice the rate of increase posted in the fourth quarter of 1979, compared with the year before. But these earnings gains for the first quarter are misleading, since they trace entirely to higher valued inventories and increased depreciation allowances. Operating profits flattened, compared with the year earlier—which figures, considering the slowing in final sales in this year's first quarter, after adjusting for inflation."

In other words, in the bank's view, the cheerful consensus of the nation's leading executives was plain wrong, and it was plain wrong, at least in part, because the people at the top simply couldn't manage to get a clear reading of their own profitability. The average consumer, it seems, was less myopic.

Still more lamentable than the myopia evident in the executive suite is the fogginess manifested by so many people who are actually in the business of forecasting the investment outlook. A "sentiment index of leading investment services," assembled regularly by Goldman, Sachs & Co. of New York, measures the percentage of investment advisory services deemed "bearish" about the stock market. Traced back to the early 1960s, the index repeatedly has grown more bearish after—not before—general declines in stock prices. By the same token, bullishness has often been most prevalent precisely when the stock market has been in the early stages of a sharp decline.

Example: In early 1977 fewer than 10 percent of the advisory services were deemed bearish about the market outlook—a near record-low percentage. And yet in the ensuing year the Dow Jones industrial average fell from nearly 1000 to about 750; when the average subsequently began to bounce back to nearly 900 in early 1978, more than 60 percent of the advisers were regarded as bearish about the market outlook.

Top executives aren't alone in their failure to assess the profit picture accurately. A study of Cyrus J. Lawrence Inc., a New York investment concern, matches actual earnings results of particular corporations against the preliminary estimates of leading investment analysts. The Lawrence firm has averaged, for instance, estimates of analysts at leading institutions for the first quarter of 1980 against estimates for the comparable period a year earlier. The average estimate for Aluminum Co. of America, for example, was that its first quarter per-share earnings would drop 15.4 percent. In fact, they rose 12.2 percent. Other outstanding goofs from the seventeen corporations covered in the report: CBS Inc. was estimated at minus less than 1 percent and actually was down 26.6 percent; Exxon was guessed at plus 24.2 percent and was up 103.7 percent; Texas Instruments was estimated at plus 14.6 percent and was up 31 percent.

The most prestigious forecasters within the business community, of course, are economists. They attempt to set a framework within which stock analysts can shape their recommendations.

How accurately have these seers managed to divine the economy's broad course? The answer must be that, by and large, the track records are unimpressive. Some years, to be sure, have proved trickier than others to foresee. Particularly difficult for most economists was 1979. The consensus as that year approached was for a mild downturn followed by a recovery around year's end. In fact, no downturn occurred in 1979. But a recession did begin in January of 1980, precisely when the consensus believed that a recovery would begin.

Business Week magazine, discussing the forecasting of economists in the early months of 1980, concluded that, under the circumstances, "the best thing that businessmen can do is take their order books and the economic news more seriously than ... their economists." The article cited two particularly unfortunate performances by establishment forecasters—Albert T. Somers, chief economist of the Conference Board, and Morris Cohen, then economist of Schroder, Naess & Thomas, a Wall Street investment concern. Mr. Somers, the report noted, originally had expected a serious recession in 1980, but in April of that year, with evidence of recession seemingly skimpy, he, along with some others, switched gears, proclaiming that "it's inflation, not a recession, that is spectacularly documented in the incoming data." In fact, the economy was already sliding into a severe recession and the price spiral was easing.

Mr. Cohen was among the few forecasters who correctly predicted that no recession would develop during 1979. However, the article recalled, he made the painful mistake of producing a similarly sanguine forecast for 1980. In mid-March, with business activity sharply declining, the forecaster was still maintaining that the economy would expand in every single quarter of 1980.

"Not only have economists missed the intensity and timing of each of the seven postwar recessions," stated *Business Week*, "but their forecasts seem to be getting worse, even as their acceptance by policy makers and businessmen rises."

Unhelpful Uncle

Altogether, we see that the average investor has virtually nowhere to turn for investment aid. What about the government? Uncle Sam, sad to relate, has managed over many years to generate misery aplenty for investors. Consider, if you will, the matter of government savings bonds. How often has the government urged citizens to buy savings bonds? Anyone so trusting as to heed such advice has usually been badly burned.

For almost forty years, Uncle Sam has been pushing, as a sound, long-term investment, various denominations of low-interest U.S. savings bonds. Yet it's difficult to imagine many unwiser investments. At a 7 percent rate of inflation, for example, the typical savings bond return was wiped out by the price spiral through much of the 1970s. With inflation at twice that rate, as it often has been, savings bond buyers stand to lose half their investment's purchasing power within a decade.

Noting such statistics, Robert M. Bleiberg, editor of *Barron's* magazine, has observed: "In the relentless quest to raise money, Big Brother, with fine irony, doesn't blink at exploiting those who, for whatever reason, lack the resources or know-how to protect themselves; wrapped in the flag though it be, it's bad government and . . . bad business." He concludes: "The Secretary of the Treasury should actively seek Congressional authority to either eliminate the savings bond program or raise interest rates to market levels." Instead, government advertising campaigns, playing on Americans' desire to gain long-term financial security on the one hand and on their patriotism on the other, frequently have tried to inveigle investors into buying more and more of these unwise securities.

One shouldn't trust Uncle Sam as an investment adviser. Nor, we might add, is it wise to assume that the government is likely to protect John Q. Public against supposedly unsound investments. My disastrous investment in Home-Stake Production, for example, was made only after I had ascertained that the firm's prospectus had been reviewed by the Securities and Exchange Commission (SEC). Never again will I use that endorsement as any sort of an investing safeguard or guide.

While claiming to be safeguarding investors, the government has occasionally managed in fact to work against the interests of innocent individuals. A horrendous illustration of this involves a maverick money manager, whom I once profiled on the front page of *The Wall Street Journal*. He was, of all things, a West Point graduate and a retired Army colonel. The late Col. Edward C. Harwood for years had been steering his clients away from the sort of investments that Citibank, for example, admired. He correctly anticipated a worsening price spiral and kept steering people into Swiss franc-based investments and gold-mining stocks. Both proved to be magnificent suggestions. However, the colonel turned out to be less than thorough in such mundane matters as registering properly with the various regulatory authorities that oversee the investment-advisory business. Unfortunately, my front page write-up of his successful activities, conducted from a beautiful home in rolling country near Great Barrington, Massachusetts, caught the eye of various regulators. It developed that certain registration requirements hadn't been properly met. Shortly thereafter, the SEC charged the colonel with various irregularities and sought a court order to liquidate his clients' holdings. Without admitting or denying the charges, Colonel Harwood in August of 1976 signed a consent order which, in effect, barred him from the securities business.

Among other things, the SEC charged that these "hapless" investors had been induced into parting with their money by "false and misleading statements about the impending collapse of the U.S. and world economies" and by "glowing promises of . . . high profits and tax benefits and safe investments tied to gold." At the SEC's behest, the court in Washington appointed both special auditors to go over the colonel's books and "guardians" in the United States and Switzerland, effectively freezing clients' assets.

All this was done, of course, in the name of "protecting" investors. But in reality, the interests of investors were jeopardized by the SEC action. None of the colonel's four thousand clients had complained about the alleged irregularities charged by the government. Yet, on account of the government suit, the Harwood-managed assets were frozen over a prolonged period, in which the price of gold skidded—to as low as $103 an ounce from around the $200 level when the "protection" effort was initiated.

Gold prices, of course, eventually soared far above the $200-per-ounce mark, and clients of the colonel who stuck by his advice prospered greatly. They would not have done so, however, had another of the SEC's recommendations been agreed to in court—that Harwood clients sell out their gold holdings at a price of around $150 an ounce or below and the proceeds be placed in Treasury securities, yielding some 7.5 percent annually.

Irwin Borowski, associate director of the SEC's enforcement division, at the time defended the recommendation on the ground that the colonel's clients were mainly "elderly . . . poor, innocent people who . . . don't understand the fraudulent nature of the securities they were offered initially" and that they had been "brainwashed by a constant stream of mailings about gold and gold stocks."

The lesson of the Harwood case, it seems, is that the average investor needs protection not from the Edward Harwoods of the country, but from governmental "protectors."

6.
On
My
Own

It may be comforting to believe that success or failure in a particular endeavor depends to a very large degree, if not entirely, on effort and a reasonable amount of intelligence. But the plain truth is that often things may hinge mainly on a huge imponderable—dumb luck. This was the situation when with considerable uncertainty, as described in Chapter 2, I finally took my leave of the investment gentlemen at Citibank and decided to do some portfolio managing on my own. Unaccustomed to doing it myself—and doing it against the best advice of a prestigious establishment bank—I needed a bit of moral support, of go-ahead-and-do-it, of follow-your-instincts.

Perry Flynn was my element of luck. When I chanced to meet him in early 1973, through a mutual stockbroker friend for whom Perry worked, I had already concluded that I should in all likelihood sell various stocks that had been acquired during my London absence—the Sears, the Southland, the Continental Telephone, the IBM, the Avon. What I needed, of course, was a shove, an unhesitating word of encouragement to do it. And that is precisely what I got from Perry Flynn. Do it, he told me, and don't wait about.

These sales, as noted in Chapter 2, were made in May of

1973, a time when the American economy was still expanding at a healthy clip. A time of such economic growth would hardly seem to justify the sort of no-confidence about the outlook that Perry and I shared. However, it developed that each of us had arrived at our relatively gloomy assessments of investment prospects—particularly for such stocks as Citibank's choices—through similar routes. In brief, we each had a wary eye on something that apparently had been forgotten by much of the country's economic establishment—the ups and downs of the business cycle.

Precisely how the business cycle works will be discussed presently. Suffice it for now to say that the American economy, throughout its existence, has expanded unsteadily from year to year, in cyclical fashion. For a while, general business activity is in an up-phase. This ends and a down-phase takes over, characterized by rising unemployment, sliding corporate profits, and, by no coincidence, skidding stock prices. Then another up-phase begins, and the cycle repeats. It is only because the up-phases generally are longer and more pronounced than the down-phases that today's economy is larger and more prosperous than that which existed, say, a hundred years ago.

The familiar, obvious yardsticks of economic activity—gross national product (GNP), industrial output, employment, corporate profits and the like—were still shining green-for-go in the spring of 1973. Overall business, it seemed clear, was solidly within an up-phase of the business cycle. Measured in terms of the dollar's 1972 buying power, the GNP in the first quarter of 1973 was at a record level, exceeding $1.2 trillion annually, and still clearly on the rise. In twelve months, the GNP level had risen nearly $100 billion. At the same time, output of the nation's factories was leaping from record to new record. The output index was nearing 130, with the 1967 average serving as a base of 100. Barely a year earlier, around the start of 1972, the index stood only at about 110. Also bright in the spring of 1973 was the job picture. The unemployment rate, at about 5 percent of the labor force, was on the decline. As recently as the fall of 1972 it had reached nearly 6 percent. Moreover, a remarkable number of jobs was being generated in this expanding economy. Employment had just crossed the 80 million mark for the first time in U.S. history. A record 57 percent of working-age Americans held jobs, and this employment-to-population ratio seemed likely to keep climbing briskly. Not surprisingly, corporate profits in early 1973 were rising apace. The after-tax profit level crossed $60 billion in late 1972 and was near $70 billion a short six months later.

In such sunny circumstances, what in the world was bothering Perry Flynn and myself? Why were we both skittish about the sort of conventional stocks favored by my Citibank advisers? Why did we both, separately, conclude that the time had arrived to undertake an investment course that by conventional Wall Street standards seemed exceedingly peculiar?

There are several answers, but the overriding consideration for each of us was a dawning appreciation of the ups and downs of the business cycle. In May of 1973, when I unloaded all those Citibank stock recommendations, the American economy had been in an expansion phase of the business cycle for two and a half years. As up-phases of the cycle go, that's a considerable length of time. The average duration of a business expansion—there have been more than two dozen since the record keeping began in 1854—works out to roughly three years. So, in May of 1973, the length of the up-phase was already close to average.

The message from all this, for me and, as I was to discover, for Perry, was to be wary. Periods of economic expansion don't persist forever, and when one has gone on for as long as thirty months the prudent investor would seem well advised to begin looking around for recessionary storm clouds.

Where to Look?

But with all that strength in such big-headline yardsticks as GNP, factory output, jobs, and profits, where to look?

One place to look—indeed the first place where I did look hard in the spring of 1973—is at a business barometer published monthly by the Commerce Department. It's called, forbiddingly, the "Composite Index of Leading Economic Indicators." This index, composed of twelve diverse economic statistics, has foreshadowed faithfully, over many decades, the ups and downs of the economy as a whole. It has tended to begin dropping at least several months before the economy as a whole begins to decline, and it has usually started to climb again before any renewal of overall business growth.

In the spring of 1973 I noticed a disquieting fact about the leading-indicator index. While the headline-grabbing gauges of economic activity were smoothly on the rise, this barometer was dropping. The decline followed a long, steep increase that had begun four months before the pit of the 1969–70 recession. Between July of 1970 and February of 1973, the index climbed from a reading of 103.4—on a base of 1967 = 100—to a record 133.4, a 30-point rise in just two and a half years.

But then the pattern began to change. The March 1973 reading dipped to 133.2. In April still another decline occurred, as the index fell to 132.4. Clearly, the red lights were beginning to flash. While a two-month drop in the leading-indicator index by no means assures that a recession is on the way, it decidedly is cause for concern.

Concerned I was, and so, it developed, was my stockbroker friend Perry Flynn.

There was another ominous and little-noticed development that attracted our attention in the spring of 1973. Corporate profits, it goes without saying, are closely linked to stock prices. In normal circumstances, the price of a particular company's stock will tend to rise if that company's after-tax profits also rise and to decline if profits decline. After all, it is the profit picture that in the long-run generally determines how attractive a particular stock may be for an investor.

In the spring of 1973, as noted, the after-tax profits of corporations in general were rising briskly, having surpassed $60 billion for the first time in late 1972. However, the profit picture that was widely followed in 1973, and which grabbed the largest headline, was highly deceptive.

We noted in Chapter 5 that a survey of 1,600 chief executives found a high degree of "business confidence" in early 1980, precisely as the economy was nosediving into a new recession. The miscalculation, it was further observed, apparently reflected an executive inability to separate out from profit figures such illusory components as more highly valued inventories and increased depreciation allowances.

Fortunately, Washington's statistics mills each quarter provide various yardsticks by which investors may gauge the trend of corporate profits. There is the aforementioned yardstick reflecting simply the after-tax profits of corporations as a whole. This measure was unmistakably on the rise as 1973 began and, in fact, it kept right on rising briskly until about the middle of 1974, by which time the economy was mired in a severe recession and the stock market was a disaster area.

However, in early 1973, some other profit barometers were already beginning to point toward stormy-weather-ahead. One that caught my eye especially was a Commerce Department statistical series titled, once again in forbidding fashion, "Corporate Profits After Taxes with IVA and CCA."

What all that means is simply this:

The Commerce Department takes the basic profit picture—the widely followed measure that crossed $60 billion in the final quarter of 1972—and subtracts two important items from the after-tax total. One, called IVA in the jargon of the statistical bureaucracy, stands for "inventory valuation adjustment." The other, CCA, stands for "capital consumption allowance." Together, quite simply, they represent adjustments of the familiar after-tax profit total to allow for increases in the replacement costs of inventories and capital equipment. In early postwar years, when inflation was at a low, single-digit level, such adjustments were negligible. But by 1973 the price spiral was beginning to distort all sorts of barometers by which investors traditionally assess the business outlook. Accordingly, any investment adviser troubling to peruse the Commerce Department's little-noticed profit gauge in May of 1973 would have spotted a troubling development—the start of a pronounced decline. The adjusted profit rate, at some $52 billion in 1972, fell about $1 billion in the first quarter of 1973, and the measure continued dropping sharply with little interruption. By mid-1974, when the conventional profit yardstick was at a high of $80 billion, the adjusted version was down close to $20 billion.

Another generally overlooked profit barometer also was giving off a warning signal in early 1973. Based on data gathered by the Commerce Department and Bureau of Labor Statistics, the gauge is actually a ratio of two indexes—one reflecting the average price charged by nonfarm businesses and the other, the denominator, the average per-unit cost of labor in those businesses. The construction of the ratio is such that it normally serves as a sort of early, early warning system for the economy in general and for corporate profitability in particular.

Obviously, if companies' unit labor costs begin to rise far faster than they manage to raise their prices, their profitability will begin to suffer. And in early 1973 this ratio was beginning to drop. At a high of 98 in the latter months of 1972, it slipped to 97 in the first three months of 1973, to 96 in the year's second quarter, and to 95 in the third.

Seeking a Safeguard

In May 1973 the incipient decline worried me. And it worried Perry Flynn. On top of the other trouble signals that concerned us, it seemed to spell one thing—that a business slump was on the way and it well could turn out to be a rough one. Neither Perry nor I, quite obviously, possessed the gift of soothsaying and therefore we could not foresee the steep oil price boosts and the oil embargo that lay ahead. But we both were convinced that, whatever might happen for better or worse on the political front in coming months, the ingredients for a downphase in the business cycle were already taking shape. The only question that remained for us was the straightforward matter of how best to safeguard an investment nest egg in the face of a severe oncoming slump in general business activity.

We knew that the stock market, where my particular nest egg in large measure resided, had served poorly over the years as an investment sanctuary when recessionary clouds were gathering. The remarkable connection between stock-price movements and the ups and downs of the business cycle will be discussed in detail later. Suffice it now to note that the stock market—as reflected in the Standard & Poor's index of 500 common stocks—is among the twelve components of the aforementioned index of leading economic indicators compiled each month by the Commerce Department. Indeed, the S&P index in 1973 was ranked by the National Bureau of Economic Research, the nonprofit business study group, as the most reliable of the twelve component indicators. Up to that time in the post-World War II era, the stock-price index had invariably begun to drop some months before the onset of down-phases in the business cycle, to fall sharply during the early months of each down-phase, and then, again leading the general economy, to rise sharply with the approach of the next up-phase of the cycle.

Clearly, the message for me in all this was to sell the stocks which Citibank, with its discretionary authority, had recently acquired. As we will see later, buy-sell decisions in the stock market depend on more than merely business-cycle considerations. Particular stock issues, for instance, may be especially cheap in terms of earnings, or have especially bright prospects, or tend to fare well when the economy generally faces trouble, or be subject if sold to huge capital-gains taxes. Such factors must be weighed carefully and can on occasion militate against a sale even in the face of an approaching recession.

In fact, none of these considerations applied in the case of Sears or Continental Telephone or Southland or IBM or Avon. None could possibly be regarded as cheap in terms of its dividend return to investors; I have already noted the scanty dividend yield of the new selections. None had earnings prospects that could be deemed bright in the face of a recessionary business climate, and certainly none fit into any category of stock that had traditionally fared well as the economy was starting to sink. And, in the relatively short time since each had been purchased, there most assuredly were no pressing capital-gains tax concerns on my part. As noted in Chapter 2, three of the five issues were sold—miraculously, in retrospect—at a slight profit. But losses in the other two issues approximately offset the three gains.

I should perhaps observe here, parenthetically, that the earlier sales that Citibank transacted while it possessed discretionary authority—particularly the sales of Continental Oil and Standard of California—did indeed involve a significant capital gain. The importance of tax considerations in setting an investment strategy will be taken up in Chapter 16; however, it's worth noting here that tax considerations—which I had good reason to believe never entered the minds of the Citibank counselors—constituted still another argument against the portfolio switching that was nonetheless undertaken.

To sell a stock for $100 that cost $100 will net you no capital gain on the transaction quite obviously, and therefore will entail no tax obligation. You are left with the full $100 sale proceeds to plow into some other investment if you choose. But if the stock that you sell for $100 cost you, say, $50, you will have gained $50 on the transaction. You won't have $100 to reinvest, but $100 minus the capital-gains tax due on the $50 gain. The precise amount of the tax obligation will vary according to your tax bracket, and in any event won't normally exceed 20 percent of the gain, provided that the security sold had been yours for at least a year.

In May of 1973, of course, there was little that could be done to rectify any of these earlier mistakes. With the Avon and other issues sold, and a major recession apparently on the way, the question left was simply: Where, with safety uppermost, should the new cash be put?

The investment decision turned out to be remarkably easy to make. Only a little common sense was needed. Stock prices, we have seen from the S&P index, tend to go down when a recession is coming on. Other indexes show a similar tendency for bond prices. So, quite obviously, logic in early 1973 militated against stock or bond investments. The commodity game, as we will see in Chapter 14, involves large risks and normally isn't any place for nest-egg money. Much the same thing can be said about real-estate investing. By a simple process of elimination, we concluded that a large portion of the new cash should remain as cash in a form that would provide a decent level of interest. The particular vehicle used was the Treasury bill, a short-term federally guaranteed security whose yield is exempt from state and local taxation and over prolonged periods has served to offset, at least partly, erosion of the dollar's buying power caused by inflation.

Since the offset was expected to be only partial, and since some selective stocks do tend to fare well when business generally is souring, logic dictated a further move—to invest a fraction of the new cash in gold-mining securities. Such shares often have performed better than average when times turn bad. And in early 1973 they seemed to provide an additional attraction—a tendency to rise as inflation worsened, and in early 1973 inflation certainly was becoming worse.

So that was it—a recession-proof nest egg comprising cash, or rather its Treasury-backed equivalent, and a modest investment in gold-mining stocks. It might have seemed to many a gamble at the time to turn away from blue-chip names endorsed by the country's economic establishment and instead to sit with cash and a few shares of stock in some tongue-twisting gold-mining operations in South Africa about which I knew little. However, as things turned out, I emerged from the 1973–75 recession in better shape financially than when I entered it. During it, I might note, the S&P stock index plunged nearly 50 percent and the dollar's buying power shriveled.

In retrospect, it's clear that one central factor can be credited for my fortunate investment moves in 1973—a new appreciation of the business cycle and its inevitable impact on investing. By the same token, I'm convinced that an essential neglect of business-cycle considerations explains how such institutions as Citibank could allow a Sears or an Avon to reside in the portfolio of a middle-income client in early 1973. The fixation with the "growth" potential of such issues apparently was overriding. Respected investment advisers, it seemed, convinced themselves that such "growth" stocks were well-nigh impervious to the constraints that can develop in a down-phase of the business cycle. I should add that Perry Flynn's concern in early 1973 about business-cycle prospects, so similar to mine, was by no means widely shared, even among relatively small Wall Street securities firms that hardly typified the financial establishment. Indeed, Perry's own colleagues generally maintained a far more sanguine view of the stock-market outlook in early 1973, to a degree where Perry's gloominess stamped him as something of a doomsayer. The gloom of Perry Flynn was very shortly, however, to prove entirely warranted.

William Tehan remarked, as noted in Chapter 4, that between 1962 and 1965 he became intrigued with the workings of the business cycle and its impact on investing and that he read extensively about it. My discovery of the importance of the business cycle came later, but I was no less impressed than Mr. Tehan with the cycle's significance to investing. Indeed, I would submit that the first step toward investment independence—the capacity to do it sensibly yourself—demands a basic understanding of just what the business cycle is and how to keep a tab on it. As we will discover, that procedure is a good deal simpler than one might suppose.

7.
Longer Trends

THE UP-PHASES AND DOWN-PHASES OF THE BUSINESS CYCLE REMAIN at the crucial center of any prudent investment technique. Recessions and recovery periods never should be disregarded in any effort to make the most of one's financial resources.

However, this essential consideration does not mean that secular developments may safely be ignored. "Secular" in this context, according to Mr. Webster, suggests a very long term, a tendency that transcends merely a year or two or three and rather unfolds from one generation to the next and, perhaps, to the next. Precisely because so long an interval is involved, secularity can be difficult to spot. Yet, the ability to detect such long-term tendencies can spell the difference between investment success and failure.

Let us ponder, for example, the matter of inflation. Its persistent rise through much of the post-World War II era clearly constitutes a secular phenomenon. Any individual who appreciates the ways in which the ups and downs of the business cycle can affect various facets of the economic scene is well prepared to invest wisely. But that individual will be wiser still if he or she also appreciates long-term developments, quite apart from the business cycle, that are at work as well.

We will show in the next chapter how the ups and downs of the business cycle influence the inflation rate. You will see, for instance, that inflation is relatively severe near the end of a business-cycle up-phase and often at its very worst in the initial months of a recession. You also will see that, as a recession deepens, the rate of price increase begins to decline and keeps dropping right through the early months of the ensuing business cycle up-phase. Thereafter, as the up-phase keeps progressing, inflation once again worsens.

With this knowledge of the relationship between the business cycle and inflation, you will be able to understand, for example, that investments tending especially to be hurt by inflation will logically fare worst around the onset of a recession and best around the start of a recovery period. That understanding, in itself, puts you far ahead of most investors, especially the many who habitually disregard the ups and downs of the business cycle. But you will fare even better if you're also aware of the secular trend of inflation. Through the 1950s, then the 1960s, then the 1970s, and into the early 1980s—until 1982—inflation kept slowly worsening. The rate of price increase, it's true, tended to ease over the course of each recession. However—and this is the point to bear in mind—with each new up-phase of the cycle, the inflation rate started to move back up again from a somewhat higher level than existed around the beginning of the preceding business-cycle up-phase.

In short, focusing on the secular pattern, you would see that inflation, while responding as usual to the ups and downs of the business cycle, was also growing stickier with each new phase of the business cycle. And, appreciating this, you would logically make an effort, very wisely, to eschew investments particularly affected by inflation—even if business-cycle experience suggested otherwise. You might, for instance, resist a temptation, understandable from a business-cycle viewpoint, to plunge into public-utility securities, stocks which tend to be especially sensitive to the sort of interest-rate increases that invariably accompany any worsening of inflation.

Secular trends, then, are important and must not be neglected in one's investment strategy. And, fortunately, such long-term developments aren't really all that difficult to spot, if one simply steps back from the trees to survey the forest. The long-term rise of inflation in the United States from 1913 to 1981 is traced in Figure 1.

The long-term worsening of U.S. inflation can readily be pinpointed. The annual rate of overall price increase can be calculated for specific periods during which the economy moved through various cyclical phases. Let us begin with 1957–60 and then take 1960–66, 1966–69, 1969–73, and finally 1973–79. In 1957–60 inflation in America averaged only 1.8 percent yearly. In 1960–66 the average was very slightly higher, at 1.9 percent. In 1966–69 however, there was an appreciable jump in the rate, to 4.2 percent a year. In 1969–73 it reached 5.1 percent annually and in 1973–79, 7.7 percent.

Certainly, a closer look at the price data would show that this progression toward worsening inflation was not uninterrupted. Some months, particularly late in recessionary periods, witnessed a pronounced easing of the price spiral. But the secular pattern could hardly be plainer, at least to anyone taking the trouble to stand back and peruse the longer-term period.

An additional consideration in any attempt to glimpse developments that transcend the business cycle's ups and downs is that such developments tend to be international in scope. Using times that are roughly similar to those applied above to the United States, we find that in Britain, for instance, the annual rate of overall price increase also progressively accelerated. An average inflation rate of 2.7 percent a year in Britain in 1957–60 was followed in the succeeding four time periods by rates of 3.2, 3.6, 9, and, in 1973–79, 15.4 percent. A similar progression is evident in Japan. In the same time spans, its annual rate of inflation moved from 3.7, to 4.2, to 5.3, to 6.7, and, in 1973–79, to 7.5 percent. A similar, though slightly less pronounced, pattern shows up in West Germany, among other industrial countries. This steady worsening of inflation over more than two decades, of course, partly reflects the steep crude-oil price boosts that began in 1973, after the Arab oil em-

FIGURE 1

Consumer Prices

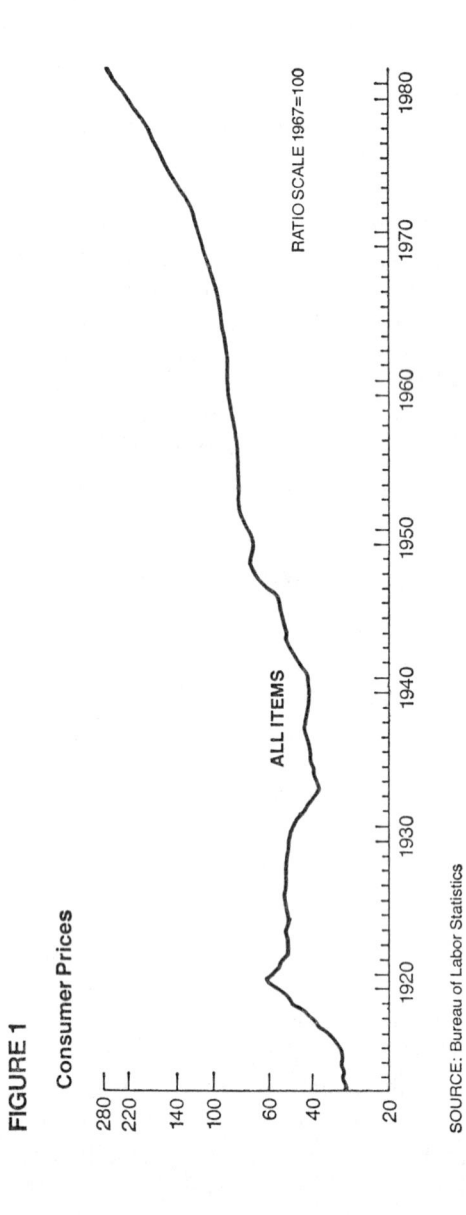

ALL ITEMS

RATIO SCALE 1967=100

SOURCE: Bureau of Labor Statistics

bargo and subsequent steep price increases imposed by the major oil-exporting countries. As the various statistics make clear, however, the upward march of the inflation rate was well along by the time 1973 rolled around. At the most, it can be said that the post-1973 oil price boosts merely exacerbated a secular development already well established.

Deep Roots

Other factors underlying the long-term inflation trend were also at work between 1957 and 1973, as well as thereafter. Arthur F. Burns, a former chairman of the Federal Reserve Board and a noted student of long-term economic trends, asserts that "the persistent inflational bias" evident in the data stems, essentially, "from the philosophic and political currents that have been transforming economic life in the United States and elsewhere since the 1930s." He maintains that Americans' "tradition of individualism" was shattered in the 1930s and 1940s, first by the Great Depression and then by the involvement in World War II. "Just as Americans were persuaded during the Depression that the federal government should help the unemployed," he states, "so they were taught by the experience of World War II to look to the government to prevent unemployment in the first place. Under the compulsions of war, the government had demonstrated that it could assure gainful employment for every willing hand; it therefore seemed reasonable—and not only to followers of [the late British economist John Maynard] Keynes—to expect government to do the same in a time of peace."

The philosophy of which Mr. Burns speaks was put into practice extensively in the early post-World War II era. The Employment Act of 1946 proclaimed the federal government's responsibility to promote "maximum employment" in the land. Later, similarly aimed legislation was passed. The Area Redeployment Act of 1961 and the Public Works Acceleration Act of 1962 were designed to develop jobs and spur business activity in areas of high joblessness. The Manpower Development and

Training Act of 1962 sought to retrain experienced workers for different jobs and train the unskilled for work. The Emergency Employment Act of 1971 established the first important public jobs program sponsored by the federal government since Great Depression years.

The cumulative effect of these and similar governmental moves was, as Mr. Burns recalls, "to impart a strong inflationary bias to the American economy." As he explains, the proliferation of governmental programs led to progressively higher tax burdens on both individuals and corporations. Even so, the former Fed chairman notes, "the willingness of government to levy taxes fell distressingly short of its propensity to spend." Between 1950 and 1981, he notes, the budget was balanced in only five years, as "the pursuit of costly social reforms often went hand in hand with the pursuit of full employment." Moreover, the economist remarks, "traditional ways of protecting particular groups against competition—such as raising farm price supports, increasing minimum wages, and imposing import quotas—did not lose their appeal as inflation kept soaring." On the contrary, all these methods of raising costs and prices were freely used, even in the face of swiftly accelerating inflation. Adding to the upward price pressure as the 1970s unfolded were multiplying governmental regulations involving such matters as health, safety, and the environment.

"However laudable in purpose," recalls Mr. Burns, "much of this regulatory apparatus was conceived in haste and with little regard to the costs being imposed on producers; substantial amounts of capital that might have gone into productivity-enhancing investments by private industry were thus diverted into uses mandated by the regulators." All the while, incentives to work diminished as various government-sponsored income maintenance plans kept expanding. Individuals, both young and old, increasingly "found it agreeable to live much of the time off unemployment insurance, food stamps, and welfare checks, perhaps supplemented by intermittent jobs in an expanding underground economy," Mr. Burns remarks.

The economist adds that "the philosophic and political currents that transformed economic life and brought on secular inflation in the United States ran strong also in other industrial countries." The rising economic expectations of people generally, along with the widespread governmental commitment to full employment, "became common features of the industrial democracies," he remarks. As a result, the secular inflation evident in the United States through much of the postwar era prevails elsewhere as well.

The investor who ignores such a long-term trend and focuses only on business-cycle developments clearly does so at his or her peril. We should add, parenthetically, that to recognize such trends as the progressive worsening of inflation hardly requires any particular expertise. The aforementioned worsening of the price spiral with successive phases of the business cycle hardly can be overlooked if one steps back from the trees. In addition, the sort of underlying considerations noted by Arthur Burns and others surely leads to a common-sense conclusion that inflation would grow more severe, rather than ease. It's a conclusion that, in the end, is judgmental. There's no simple technique of business-cycle monitoring that can provide all the investment answers. However, as Arthur Burns's analysis indicates, no stroke of genius is required to determine that inflation has long been and—notwithstanding a marked easing under the Reagan administration—threatens to continue to be the order of the day.

Germany's Misery

Somewhat trickier for investors is the important matter of determining when a secular development may have run its course. The horrendous inflation that destroyed the German economy in the early 1920s ended with startling suddenness at the end of 1923, when the existing German currency became worthless and a new unit of exchange—the *Rentenmark*—was introduced by the government. It is noteworthy that before this turn of events a remarkable deterioration occurred in the German labor situation. As late as July of 1923, the German jobless rate was less than 4 percent of the labor force. By November of the same year, as the wheels of industry ground to a halt, the jobless level approximated 30 percent, higher than any level reached during the worst months of the Great Depression in the United States.

The German investor who foresaw the sudden end of Germany's inflation in 1923 obviously enjoyed a tremendous investment advantage over those—clearly a majority of the population—who assumed that prices would keep spiraling.

Investors wondering about the U.S. price outlook in the early 1980s should keep two points in mind. First, the degree of inflation suffered in the United States and elsewhere in the latter postwar years hasn't been remotely as severe as that suffered by Germany in the early 1920s. Common sense suggests that a relatively mild rate of inflation is far likelier to persist for a long time—with interruptions, to be sure—than an extremely severe, German-style price spiral. Second, as Mr. Burns indicates, the causes of U.S. postwar inflation extend beyond simply the overproduction of money, which many historians maintained was the root cause of the German debacle.

The investor, attempting to determine roughly when the secular pattern of worsening inflation may end in the United States, would be wise to try to keep a tab on developments, mainly within the political arena, that would lead to an easing of the price spiral. There is no single signal to watch for, but there are various signs to be assessed. In a speech in September of 1979 before the directors of the International Monetary Fund in Belgrade, Arthur Burns, who had been recently replaced by Paul A. Volcker as Fed chairman, threw some light on where to be looking. "The persistent inflation that plagues the industrial democracies will not be vanquished—or even substantially curbed—until new currents of thought create a political environment in which the difficult adjustments required to end the inflation can be undertaken," he stated. "There are some signs, as yet tenuous and inconclusive," he added, "that such a change in the intellectual and political climate of the democracies is getting under way; one of the characteristic features of a democracy is that it encourages learning from experience." He went on to mention such indications of a change in climate as the introduction of pricing competition in the trucking and airline industries and a growing attention on the part of many lawmakers of the need to "strengthen incentives to work and innovate, to ways of stimulating saving and investment, to the importance of eliminating barriers to competition, to ways of reducing the regulatory burdens imposed on industry, and to other means of bolstering business confidence." At the same time, however, he cautioned that the process of winding down inflation would be a protracted affair. "American policymakers tend to see merit in a gradualist approach because it promises a return to general price stability, perhaps with a delay of five or more years, but without requiring significant sacrifices on the part of workers or their employers," he remarked. "What the very caution that leads politically to a policy of gradualism may well lead also to is its premature suspension or abandonment in actual practice."

Ultimately, investors must decide for themselves, through keeping abreast of the broad political and social climate of the time, whether a long-term trend—be it worsening inflation or proliferating crime—has about run its course. If an investor should determine for himself that inflation, for instance, will progressively ease over the next ten years or so, then quite obviously some investment decisions would be undertaken differently. Public utility stocks, for instance, could be safely and profitably played once again, according to the ups and downs of the business cycle, with little regard to secular considerations. The time to buy such interest-sensitive investments would again be nearing the pit of a down-phase of the business cycle, when inflation and interest rates would both be approaching cyclical low points.

The Debt Question

Inflation, it should be stressed, constitutes just one of a number of secular trends that astute investors may neglect only at their peril. Another, not unrelated to the progressive worsening of inflation, is the long-term growth of debt within the economy. This tendency can be seen in various ways. In 1950 household debt amounted to about 35 percent of household income. By 1960 this ratio reached nearly 65 percent. By 1970 it exceeded 70 percent. And by 1980 it topped the 80 percent level. Noting this secular pattern, Siff, Oakley and Marks Inc., a New York economic counseling concern, observed in 1980 that the lesson "for more and more people is that saving, in the traditional sense, doesn't pay, while 'saving' by borrowing (preferably to the hilt in real estate) does; only time will tell whether too many people have carried this conclusion too far."

By no coincidence, loan-delinquency rates have tended, through up-phases as well as down-phases, to climb substantially. In the quarter century from 1955 to 1980, for example, the number of consumer installment loans overdue increased from about 1.4 percent of those outstanding to more than double that rate. And, over the same span, the comparable rate for overdue conventional residential mortgages climbed from about 1 percent to more than triple that level; the ratio for overdue residential mortgages that are federally guaranteed rose even more sharply.

Households, it should be added, are by no means alone in this piling on of debt over the decades. By various yardsticks, the corporate debt burden has also soared. For example, a so-called quick ratio—corporations' current assets, less inventories, divided by their bills due within a year or less—exceeded 1.7 in the early 1960s; by the late 1970s the ratio was less than 0.9.

The rise of governmental debt, of course, is a well-known story. In the 1930s, even with the unemployment and federal budget deficits that accompanied the Great Depression, the annual interest of the U.S. government's debt averaged about $800 million a year. For the 1980s it is estimated that this interest will average more than $110 billion a year.

Peter Grace, the colorful and outspoken chief executive of W. R. Grace & Co., placed this projection in perspective during a 1979 address before a Harvard Business School group: "This annual U.S. Government interest on its debt in the 1980s is equal to $400 per minute since Columbus discovered America—and that's just for one year! Nearly $111 billion a year is a lot of billions. For instance, if a man gave his wife $1 billion and told her to spend $1,000 a day before returning home, he wouldn't see her until the year 4718. Of course, all this has taken the stuffing out of the value of the dollar. A 1930s dollar is now worth 19.6 cents. In the 1940s it took twenty-one years for the dollar to drop in half. In the 1960–70s it took fourteen years. We are in a hurry now—it takes six years at a 13.2 percent inflation rate."

Another secular trend, again not unrelated, has been pinpointed by A. Gary Shilling, mentioned earlier as an independent-minded economist who moved away from the financial establishment to set up his own consulting firm. Mr. Shilling estimated in 1977 that no fewer than 53.5 percent of the U.S. population had "their feet in the public trough." These individuals, he reckoned, are "dependent on the government in a major way for their income." The comparable foot-in-trough rate in 1960, according to the economist, was 42.3 percent. The range of individuals deemed to be dependent in a major way on the government for support included 30.3 million federal, state, and local government employees and their dependents, 19.6 million private-industry workers and their dependents, whose jobs—such as building submarines—relied on governmental spending, and finally 72.6 million recipients of government transfer payments, ranging from social security to welfare to government-subsidized housing.

Such an army of beneficiaries of governmental funds clearly won't diminish greatly overnight. At the most, its growth may slow if public concern over governmental expansion intensifies enough. The lesson is that the investor who places his bets without taking into account the government's vast, growing role—through recessions and recoveries—will be taking an unnecessary investment risk. Whatever a political leader of the moment may assert, a secular trend of such magnitude promises to persist far into the future. Thus, if business-cycle considerations should militate against holding shares in, say, a machine-tool company, you should probably think twice before selling the stock if the company also is heavily and increasingly involved in supplying products to Uncle Sam.

Growing Trade

The growth of foreign trade over the post-World War II years is another long-term development that a wise investor should bear in mind. Imports plus exports in 1980 came to roughly one quarter of the U.S. gross national product, with each trade category amounting to about one half of the total percentage. A decade earlier, the comparable figure was only about 12 percent, with each category, again, representing about one half. This long-term growth of foreign trade is obviously a phenomenon that can affect investments. An investment decision based purely on domestic business-cycle considerations might suggest, for example, that the time was ripe for buying into the U.S. auto or steel industry. But a glance at the growth of imports would quickly signal that long-term investment in those two industries could suffer from their apparent inability to compete with lower-cost autos and steel products made abroad.

It should be mentioned, with regard to particular industries, that wide disparities in performance emerge when one stands back from day-to-day events and inspects the larger picture. America's problem in spurring productivity within the economy in general has been well publicized. The long-term picture over the postwar era has been one of narrowing advances in hourly output. However, a study by the New York Federal Reserve Bank turns up much diversity within the broad pattern. It breaks the productivity picture down into ten key business areas—mining, construction, manufacturing, transportation, communications, public utilities, wholesale trade, retail trade, finance-insurance-real estate, and miscellaneous services. Then it calculates the average annual productivity advance in each category for 1948–67 and for 1967–78. For all ten businesses taken as a whole, productivity gains narrowed from 2.5 percent in 1948–67 to 1.8 percent in 1967–78. But in one category—communications—productivity gains actually were half a point larger, at 5.9 percent annually, in 1967–78 than in 1948–67. In another key category—manufacturing—productivity advanced 2.6 percent annually in both periods, so that there was no slowdown. And in three other categories—transportation, wholesale trade, and miscellaneous services—the slowdown in the 1967–78 period amounted to no more than 0.3 percent. The only categories, in fact, where a major deterioration in productivity was apparent—in each case productivity actually fell in 1967–78—were mining and construction.

Again, the lesson for investors is to be aware of long-term trends, as well as the fact that remarkable diversity may be occurring within the broad pattern.

Thus far in this chapter, we have focused on secular developments, as distinct from the shorter, familiar ups and downs of the business cycle. While the business cycle, with its ups and downs, seems likely to persist indefinitely, given human fallibility, secular trends aren't likely to go on forever. Moreover, there is a third area of concern for anyone wishing to keep tabs on long-term developments that could affect investment strategy. Over many years, various economic studies suggest that there exist other, longer cycles that transcend the recessions and recoveries that come along every few years. The most noteworthy of these is called the "Kondratieff wave."

The Kondratieff Wave

The Kondratieff wave is named for Nicolai Dimitrievich Kondratieff, a Russian economist whose major work appeared in the 1920s. Later, he was banished by Joseph Stalin, the Soviet dictator, to Siberia, where he worked in salt mines for many years and finally died. He is mentioned by Alexander I. Solzhenitsyn in *The Gulag Archipelago* as having finished his days in "solitary confinement," where he "became mentally ill . . . and died." Stalin banished Kondratieff because the Soviet economist formulated a theory which stated, in effect, that Western capitalistic economies every half century or so would invariably fall into deep depressions. This hardly sounds like the sort of doctrine that would antagonize a Communist dictator. However, Kondratieff also foresaw a self-cleansing process of renewal during these periodic capitalistic slumps that would enable the system to revive and once again flourish. What, precisely, did the Russian economist anticipate?

Basically, he suggested that economic activity in the capitalist West assumes a sort of rhythmic, wavelike behavior over very long periods. Employing price indexes and other statistics, chiefly drawn from the number mills of such relatively forward economies as the United States, France, and the United Kingdom, the Russian concluded that a "super" business cycle exists. Now referred to as the "Kondratieff wave," this supercycle supposedly extends over periods averaging approximately fifty years. Thus, a single Kondratieff cycle contains within it many of the short-term ups and downs—the recessions and the recovery periods—discussed previously.

At the heart of Kondratieff's theory is a conviction that a a very high amount of inevitability underlies economic development over the very long term. It is further assumed that governmental actions may delay or hasten these corrective interludes that will inevitably follow long periods in which economic growth has been excessive. However, it is further postulated that such actions cannot ultimately prevent these interludes from occurring. To see how this theory can be applied, its proponents cite the long history of price movements in the United States. Prices—and by no coincidence prosperity—rose substantially from the 1780s until soon after the War of 1812. Then prices declined abruptly. This constituted, according to Kondratieff theory, a "primary" recession within the supercycle. Then, until 1819, a so-called Kondratieff plateau occurred. In this time, prices declined only moderately and business activity appeared to recover somewhat. Then began a deep, "secondary" slump in which prices and economic activity dropped steeply amid proliferating unemployment and rising bankruptcies. The pit of this secondary slump was reached in the mid-1840s. This was followed by a new supercycle expansion phase, which reached a peak around the end of the Civil War, just over half a century after the War of 1812.

Kondratieff theory maintained that after the Civil War and the supercycle peak, a pattern developed that was remarkably similar to the 1812–65 pattern—a short primary recession, a plateau until 1874, a deep, long secondary slump through 1896, and finally, a sustained interval of renewed prosperity and rising prices until 1920. The price collapse and eighteen-month recession that began in July 1921, in the Kondratieff view, represented yet another primary recession within the supercycle. The balance of the 1920s reflected still another plateau period, and the Great Depression, which extended through the 1930s, marked yet another secondary slump. The renewed upturn according to proponents of the theory, persisted into the 1970s. The recession that overtook U.S. business in 1973, the most severe downturn since the Great Depression, represented still another primary recession. That downturn ended in 1975, and the 1970s decade, in the Kondratieff way of looking at things, marked one more plateau, as Figure 2 suggests.

This would suggest, of course, that the years just ahead will witness still another painful secondary slump, and that surely is a consideration for the prudent investor to bear in mind. Against it, however, should be weighed several additional thoughts. Kondratieff wave theory assumes a measure of flexibility within the U.S. economy that surely no longer exists. Unlike the situation in the primary recession of the 1920s, wages nowadays are relatively inflexible on the down side; they go up in good times far more easily than they go down in bad times. Further, Kondratieff theory does not take into account the full extent of governmental intervention in today's capitalist economies, even with the recent swing in the United States and elsewhere toward a more conservative political lead-

FIGURE 2

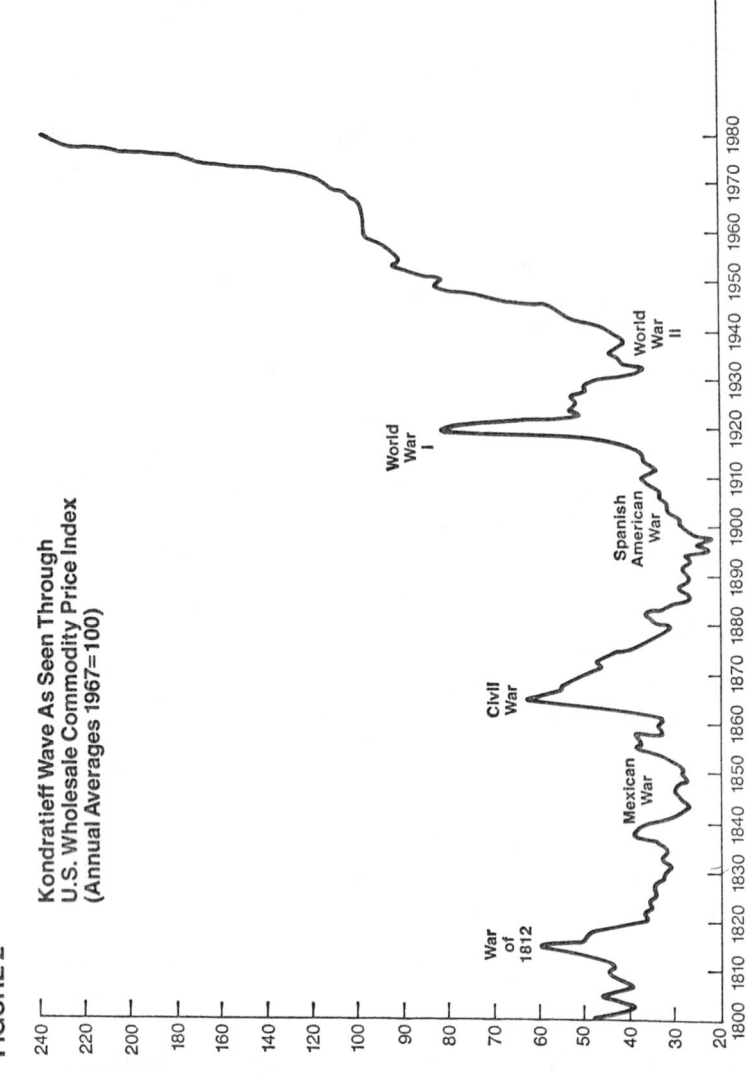

Kondratieff Wave As Seen Through U.S. Wholesale Commodity Price Index (Annual Averages 1967=100)

SOURCE: Bureau of Labor Statistics

ership. Certainly, the sharp rise of prices during the supposed plateau years, immediately after the 1973–75 recession, hardly squares with the Kondratieff precept that a primary recession will be followed by a plateau period marked by moderately declining price levels. Altogether, it can be argued, on the basis of recent U.S. economic history, that the Kondratieff wave idea is hopelessly out of touch with modern capitalism—or that the very inflexibilities appearing to invalidate Kondratieff theory could, in the years ahead, bring on a price spiral that would ultimately distort the workings of the economy so much as to cause, in the inflation's wake, still another secondary slump. Whatever does develop, the wise investor should be aware of the Kondratieff wave, taking it perhaps with a very large grain of salt, but always being watchful for signs that something more than just another down-phase of the regular business cycle may be at work.

Investors should also be aware that the Kondratieff wave is only the best known of a number of theories holding that economic activity rises and falls over periods transcending the familiar ups and downs of the business cycle. For example, there are the "Kuznets cycles," named for Simon Kuznets, an economist who taught for many years at Harvard University and was awarded the Nobel Prize in economics in 1971 for his groundbreaking work in developing ways of measuring U.S. economic activity. Kuznets cycles supposedly range up to twenty-five years, or roughly half the length of Kondratieff supercycles, and are characterized especially by swings in construction activity. Among other long-term trends that may—or may not—produce supercycles in overall economic activity, various theorists cite the impact of gold discoveries on the rate of expansion of the money supply, new technologies, the ebbs and flows of immigration, and weather patterns and their influence on food production and prices.

Investors attempting to do the job themselves should be aware that there may well be forces influencing economic activity that transcend the familiar recessions and recoveries which grab the business headlines. These longer-term considerations are important and should be kept well in mind in mapping any investment strategy. As we will see, however, the main weight must still be given to the short cycle.

In summary, the best advice is to be careful to take note of these long-term tendencies. They are important in investing—whether we are talking about inflation or debt or expanding international trade. There's no easy formula by which you will be able to deduce that, for example, the long-term growth of foreign trade is at an end and that henceforth exports will comprise a dwindling fraction of overall economic activity. Or that debt or inflation hereafter will play lesser roles in the economic picture.

The only way you can make such deductions will be by keeping abreast of the general news, out of Washington especially. That shouldn't be too difficult, however, because the secular developments that can influence your investments don't usually change direction overnight. Normally, they change course—most fortunately—with glacial slowness. If you are aware that such trends exist and monitor them with reasonable attention, it should be easy for you to spot a bona fide reversal in direction whose roots go deeper than the business cycle.

8.
Seeing
the
Cycle

IT SEEMS DIFFICULT TO BELIEVE THAT A TIME EXISTED NOT SO very long ago when a number of exceedingly influential and highly respected economists became convinced that the business cycle no longer existed in the United States. They presumed that the U.S. economy, benefiting particularly from the wise guidance supplied by policy makers in Washington, had entered a new era in which business activity would calmly keep moving to new high ground, without the nasty interruptions we have come to know as recessions.

Not surprisingly, the staunchest advocates of this new-era brand of economics were mainly to be found within the policymaking ranks in Washington. Among these self-confident individuals, for example, was a key member of President Lyndon Johnson's Council of Economic Advisers, Otto Eckstein, a Harvard professor who went on to great fortune, if not great fame, as the founding president of Data Resources Inc., a Lexington, Massachusetts, economics research organization boasting scores of wealthy corporate clients.

These new-era advocates even went so far in their heyday in the 1960s as to force a name change for an important Commerce Department publication that economists use to this day in following the business situation. The publication traces economic ups and downs, using charts and underlying statistics that extend back over many decades. Until the Johnson White House years (1964–68) the publication quite sensibly was titled *Business Cycle Developments*. However, the new-era school, with its conviction that recessions were a thing of the benighted past, could not tolerate a title suggesting that the business cycle was still around. And so, ridiculously, the Commerce Department bowed to pressure and changed the title to *Business Conditions Digest*. Serious students of the economy, relying on the publication each month, hardly cared, since for years it had been referred to as *BCD*, and the new-era title retained those same initials. It's still known among economists as simply *BCD*, but what those initials stand for now makes no reference to any sort of business cycle.

All this, of course, happened long ago and represents only a small footnote to the history of Washington's bureaucratic absurdities. However, there is a larger point that remains—namely, that it is foolish to disregard the business cycle. It will not be eliminated by changing titles of publications. Nor, for that matter, will it be erased by a constant jiggering of economic policies in an imperfect world where mistakes, by businessmen as well as Washington policy makers, will inevitably be made. Otto Eckstein, I should add, has become a fine student of the cycle's ups and downs, and the information that his firm supplies to its clients typically is replete with estimates of precisely where within the cycle the economy as a whole may stand at a particular moment.

Since those euphoric Johnson years, Mr. Eckstein, along with the rest of us, has lived through a whole series of recessions and recoveries, some far more pronounced than others, but all with an unmistakable message:

The business cycle is alive and well and living in the United States.

What do we really mean when we talk about the business cycle? What causes it? How can one follow its ups and downs? Most importantly, why is it of such importance to investors of all stripes?

Back to 1854

A cycle, very simply, constitutes a period of time occupied by a series of events that repeat themselves regularly and in the same order. Students of economic history have found that month-to-month business activity tends, like many other forms of activity, to move in cyclical fashion. Indeed, this tendency has been tracked in the U.S. economy all the way back to 1854. Since then, the economy has expanded, then contracted, then expanded again, then contracted again, and so on and so on, for decade after decade. In all, through 1980, there have been twenty-nine complete up-phases of the business cycle and, obviously, an equal number of down-phases.

Today's economy is vastly larger than that existing back in 1854. But the business cycle persists, essentially manifesting the same characteristics as it did in 1854. The National Bureau of Economic Research, based in Cambridge, Massachusetts, has tracked all the ups and downs and has found, among other things, that the average expansion period has lasted about three years and the average contraction period about a year and a half. The picture, to be sure, has varied immensely. The shortest recessionary phase was only about a half-year long, while one downturn—a monster that developed as long ago as 1879—endured for no less than sixty-five months. Similarly, expansions have lasted as briefly as ten months and as long as one hundred six months. The latter was the recovery that became known as the "Soaring Sixties." It began in February 1961 and persisted until December 1969, at which time an eleven-month recession set in.

The National Bureau of Economic Research over the years has assumed a role as official arbiter in the matter of pinning down precisely when turning points appear to have occurred in the business cycle. The National Bureau defines a business-cycle "peak" as the month when an economic up-phase ends and down-phase commences. No particular day within such a month is ever designated as the exact turning point, but for practical purposes it is assumed that midmonth marks the change of cycle. In similar fashion, the National Bureau defines a business-cycle "trough" as the month when an economic down-phase bottoms out and another up-phase gets under way. Again, midmonth marks the cycle change.

Economists at the National Bureau peruse a vast array of statistics when—usually several months after the fact—they set the month for a particular peak or trough of the cycle. The broadest available measure of overall business activity is the gross national product, which represents the marketplace value of all goods and services produced within the economy over the course of one year. This statistic, when adjusted to eliminate any distortion caused by price changes, generally has been on the rise when the economy has been in an up-phase of the cycle and on the decline during cyclical down-phases. The GNP is only the foremost of many statistics—called "coincident indicators"—that are monitored at the National Bureau in an effort to sort out the ups and downs of the business cycle. Other such indicators include, to name only a few, industrial production, consumer spending, and personal income.

Seeking the Whys

The causes of the business cycle are less easily discerned than its existence. Students of economic history, for instance, can clearly spot the cyclical ups and downs simply by casting a long look back at such business barometers as the gross national product or industrial production. But to understand the whys is a trickier business.

If human beings were perfect, we suspect, there would be no business cycle. Lyndon Johnson's economists, who imagined an unending progression of gains in business activity, would be right and that name change of BCD would be justified.

However, imperfection remains the prevailing human tendency, in economic policy making as elsewhere. The business cycle exists because planners in private businesses, as well as in Washington's halls of power, make mistakes. When business is bad, they believe that it will remain bad indefinitely. Disheartened businessmen give up the ghost, running down their inventories and stripping their employment rolls just when they should be getting set for renewed economic growth. By the same token, politicians launch vast new pump-priming schemes, in the name of halting a recession that has already ended. All this happens too late—not when economic activity is weakening and stimulative measures would be timely, but when the economy is naturally on the mend and needs little or no additional attention.

Conversely, when business has been faring well, there is a tendency, entirely human and understandable, to assume that the good times will go on forever. Businesses, believing the market to be insatiable, inevitably acquire unsustainable supplies that will prove far in excess of reasonable demand. Meanwhile, within the policy-making area, concern mounts that inflation, aggravated by shortages in the face of an ever-rising demand for goods and services, must be brought to heel. The monetary and fiscal brakes slam down—too hard, of course, so that what should have been a gentle slowing of the rate of economic growth becomes instead still another nasty contraction of general business activity, marked as usual by rising unemployment, falling profits, and other unpleasantness.

The fact that human error perpetuates the business cycle, it should be added, does not mean that the timing of the ups and downs remains impervious to events. An extreme example occurred in 1973. The fall of that year marked the first oil squeeze that the Arab nations imposed on the major industrial countries, including the United States. At the time of the imposition, the U.S. economy was clearly still in an up-phase cycle that had commenced approximately three years earlier. In retrospect, it seems reasonably certain that this up-phase might well have persisted into 1974 had the oil squeeze—the embargo and the sharp price increases—not taken place. The record books show that a severe, sixteen-month recession began in November 1973. But most economists are convinced that, without the oil squeeze, the period of expansion would probably have gone on for nearly another year. My own guess is that the turning down of the economy would have begun around August of 1974. The point to bear in mind, however, is that forces were already gathering back in 1973 that would eventually have brought an end to the three-year expansion, regardless of the oil situation. For example, data from Washington made clear that, as 1973 unfolded, many businesses were beginning to accumulate unrealistically high levels of inventory. This was apparent, among other places, in a statistic issued monthly by the Commerce Department, and published in *Business Conditions Digest*. It expresses business inventories in terms of business sales. In early 1973, *BCD* informed us that this inventory-to-sales ratio stood at about 1.5, a level that historically has been associated with healthy economic growth. However, in early summer the ratio began rising, slowly at first, then more swiftly. Within a year it was close to 1.7, and it approximated 1.8 before the 1973–75 recession finally subsided.

Not All That Difficult

The apparent inability of businesses and policy makers in Washington to remain abreast of the business cycle is all the more lamentable when one considers that following the ups and downs—even anticipating them—isn't all that difficult a procedure. We noted, for example, that certain broad coincident indicators can provide an ongoing picture, albeit slightly after the fact, of precisely where the economy stands each month. While the magnitudes may vary from up-phase to up-phase and from down-phase to down-phase, certain characteristics can be found again and again. The broad behavior of the gross national product has been noted, but the behavior of all sorts of other, somewhat narrower, barometers is predictable as well. These disparate patterns of individual indicators can be glimpsed, for instance, in a close review of five recessions that hit the U.S. economy during a twenty-year period beginning in 1953.

SEEING THE CYCLE

The peak-to-trough declines in GNP, stripped of inflation, amounted to 2.7 percent in 1953–54, to 2.5 percent in 1957–58, to 0.3 percent in 1960–61, to 0.6 percent in 1969–70, and to a steep 5.7 percent in 1973–74. With this perspective, it is enlightening to observe the behavior of other key economic barometers during the five downturns in that twenty years. Overall consumer spending, also stripped of inflationary "growth," fell 0.5 percent in the 1953 recession, 1.2 percent in 1957–58, only 0.3 percent in the 1960 slump, 0.8 percent in the 1970 recession, and 2.3 percent in 1973–75. Interestingly, the comparable decline in consumer spending for durable goods—autos, appliances, and the like—turns out to have been generally more pronounced. For the same years, such spending fell 0.5, 6.9, 9, 7.9, and 9.9 percent. Sharper still, the records show, were the comparable drops in fixed-investment spending by businesses—3.9, 14.8, 4.5, 8, and 16.6 percent. And most severe of all, we see, were the declines in each recession of corporations' after-tax profits, again adjusted for inflation. In the same sequence of years the profit figure dropped 24.7, 23.6, 14.5, 34.7, and 57.3 percent.

Besides the disparate behavior of these different sectors of the broad economic picture, it should also be kept in mind that the particular peaks and troughs for many barometers may differ from those for the economy as a whole established by analysts at the National Bureau of Economic Research.

These differences in timing may seem to complicate the business-cycle picture. However, as we will observe, they also provide a key to prudent business-cycle investing, a means to riding safely, if you will, aboard the roller-coaster economy. The different behavior of different indicators allows us to anticipate turning points in the cycle, as well as the likely behavior of particular stocks, bonds, commodities, or other investment vehicles during particular phases of the cycle.

If the coincident indicators allow us to see the economy as it stands, another set of indicators—the leading indicators, in the jargon of economists—allows us to look ahead and detect where —up, down, or sideways—overall economic activity is heading.

9. Keeping Ahead of the Cycle

Leading business indicators, as these precursors of the economy's ups and downs are called, do not command headlines to the extent that broader measures of economic activity do. Unemployment jumps, and it is a large story on the TV news. The consumer price index drops, and it's on the front page. Industrial production soars, and it grabs headlines.

But how often do you see on a front page the latest report on the length of the average work week in manufacturing? Or the inflation-adjusted volume for new orders of consumer durable goods? Or the inflation-adjusted volume of new contracts and orders for plant-and-equipment facilities? Or the percentage of companies reporting slower goods deliveries? Or the rate at which new businesses are being formed? Or the net change, again adjusted for inflation, of inventories in hand or on order?

Don't feel badly if you have never even heard most of these statistical series. They remain a relatively obscure breed of economic data. All are so-called leading indicators. And they possess a most valuable attribute. Time and again, they have tended to rise months before the economy in general has turned up from a recession and, conversely, to fall before recessions have set in. Because they share this ability, despite their relative obscurity, these business barometers actually are of far greater concern to the forward-looking investor than are, say, the consumer price index or the unemployment rate. As this book will emphasize and reemphasize, a keen awareness of the movement of the business cycle—its stage and its direction—is absolutely vital to investing wisely. And, as noted, this awareness has been a missing ingredient responsible in large measure for the sort of investment blunders habitually committed by supposedly astute members of the financial establishment.

A First Step

A first step in keeping tabs on the leading indicators is to recognize them and to understand how each possesses distinctive characteristics. This may be accomplished, quite simply, by perusing a copy of the Commerce Department publication mentioned earlier, *Business Conditions Digest*.

Copies of *BCD*, which is published monthly, are available, among other places, at the various field offices that the Commerce Department maintains in major cities around the country. It may also be obtained by mail from the Superintendent of Documents, U.S. Government Printing Office, Washington, D.C., 20402.

The publication, in the main, is made up of statistical series that examine the past and present performance of the U.S. economy. These series, in turn, are classified according to their typical relationship with the business cycle. Using charts that extend back over much of the post-World War II period and with down-phases of the business cycle shaded, *BCD* pinpoints the characteristics of each statistical series—how it behaves when a recession lies ahead, when business is slumping, when a recovery is on the way, or when a sustained economic expansion is in progress. A typical page of *BCD* is depicted in Figures 3 and 4.

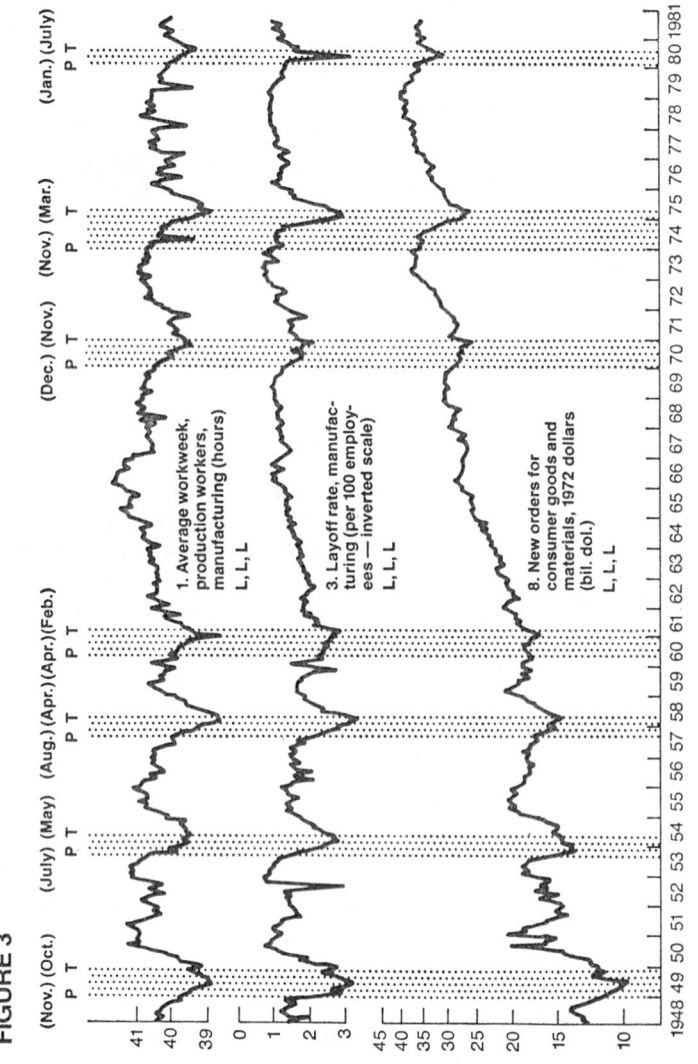

FIGURE 3

KEEPING AHEAD OF THE CYCLE 87

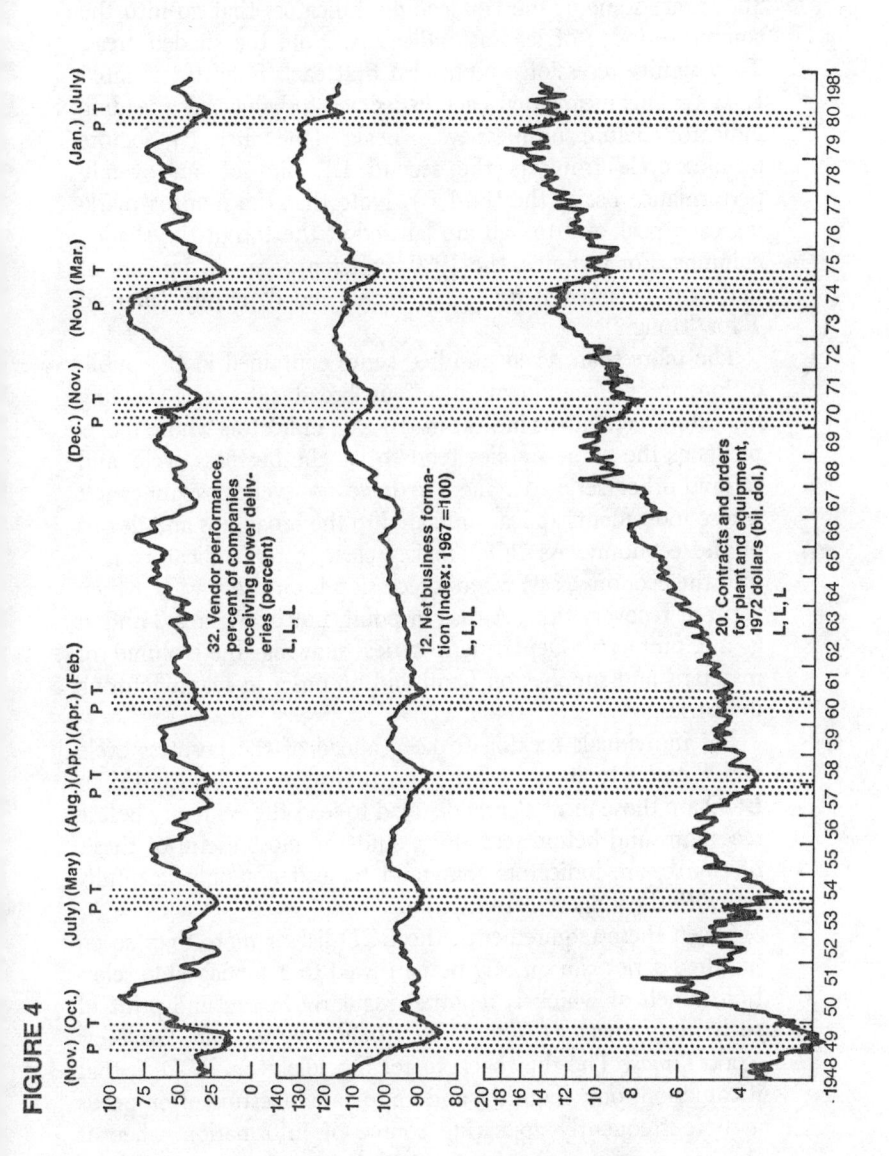

FIGURE 4

Shown are some of the key leading indicators that go into the composite index of leading indicators. Note the shaded areas. They signify recessions. Note also that each indicator is rated L, L, L. This means that each is deemed to behave as a leading indicator before business-cycle peaks (the first L), before business-cycle troughs (the second L), and on an overall-performance basis (the third L). Note that the months marking each peak and trough are labeled at the top of the shaded columns. For instance, the 1980 recession began in January of that year (marked P for "peak") and ended in July (marked T for "trough").

The more than seven hundred series contained in the publication are broken down into four broad categories—leading indicators, coincident indicators, lagging indicators whose movements as the name implies tend to lag the business cycle, and various other series, deemed to have no cyclical significance, whose movements appear unrelated to the broad ups and downs of the economy. As BCD makes clear, some indicators may lead the economy, say, when a recession is on the way, but then lag it at recovery time. A case in point, not in Figures 3 and 4, is a Commerce Department series showing the volume of materials and supplies on hand and on order in manufacturing industries.

For individuals seeking to keep ahead of the business cycle and thereby to invest wisely, the indicators to be studied in BCD are those most clearly deemed to lead the economy before recessions and before recoveries. And the most useful of these, of course, are indicators that tend to lead not only faithfully but with the longest warning time.

Given these requirements, the BCD list of more than seven hundred series can quickly be narrowed to a manageable selection, much of which is reported regularly in the fine print of such newspapers as *The Wall Street Journal* and the New York *Times*. The drawback to relying solely on BCD is that it comes out only monthly, and up-to-date investing often needs a more frequently appearing source of information when it comes to monitoring the leading indicators. If a particular indicator appears in the *Journal,* for example, at the beginning of the month but your BCD doesn't arrive until the end of the month, you obviously had better keep an eye on the *Journal* as well as on BCD.

What to Watch

What are the leading indicators that should be closely watched?

Over the years, economists have found twelve statistical series, all within the covers of BCD, to be particularly valuable as leading indicators. These include the several indicators, such as the length of the average workweek, mentioned and shown at the beginning of this chapter. But the list also includes such series as new building permits for private housing units, changes in prices of goods deemed especially sensitive to changes in demand levels, and changes in liquid assets, defined as including such savings-type items as currency, demand deposits, time deposits, savings bonds, negotiable certificates of deposit, short-term marketable U.S. securities, open-market paper, federal funds, repurchasing agreements, and money-market funds.

Still other faithful precursors of the economy's ups and downs include the inflation-adjusted money supply; stock prices, with a caveat that will be subsequently explained; the so-called accession rate within manufacturing industries, or, in plainer English, the rate at which new employees are being hired; an index of "consumer sentiment" compiled quarterly by the Survey Research Center at the University of Michigan; the number of new private-housing units started each month; the inflation-adjusted volume of residential fixed investment put in place each quarter; after-tax corporate profits; after-tax corporate profits per dollar of sales in manufacturing industries; the ratio of average prices within the economy's nonfarm business sector to labor costs per unit of output; net changes in the volume of mortgage debt outstanding; net changes in bank loans to businesses; net changes in the amount of consumer installment debt outstanding; on an inverted basis, the volume of current liabilities of business failures; and the rate at which consumer installment loans are delinquent thirty days or more.

Obviously, it would be impractical to monitor, on a regular basis, so many indicators. Accordingly, we must narrow the list to a selection of gauges proved to be not only reliable, but particularly farseeing.

The Composite of Leaders

The Commerce Department's composite index of twelve leading indicators, which is published near the end of each month and appears in such newspapers as *The Wall Street Journal* and the New York *Times*, provides a reasonable idea of just how precursive the typical leading indicator is, as the chart in Figure 5 suggests. In the twenty years from 1953 to 1973, the U.S. economy lapsed into five recessions—as noted earlier, in 1953–54, in 1957–58, in 1960–61, in 1969–70, and in 1973–75. Each recession, of course, was followed by an up-phase of the business cycle. The warning times provided by the Commerce Department's composite index—the number of months elapsing between the start of a sustained downturn in the composite index and the onset of a recession—amounted to four months before the 1953–54 recession, as much as twenty-three months before the 1957–58 recession, eleven months before the 1960–61 recession, eleven months again before the 1969–70 recession, and nine months before the 1973–75 recession. The lead times were appreciably shorter before the respective recovery periods, which is hardly a surprise in view of the fact that recessions tend to last a much shorter time than expansion phases of the business cycle.

The composite index turned up six months before the re-

KEEPING AHEAD OF THE CYCLE

FIGURE 5

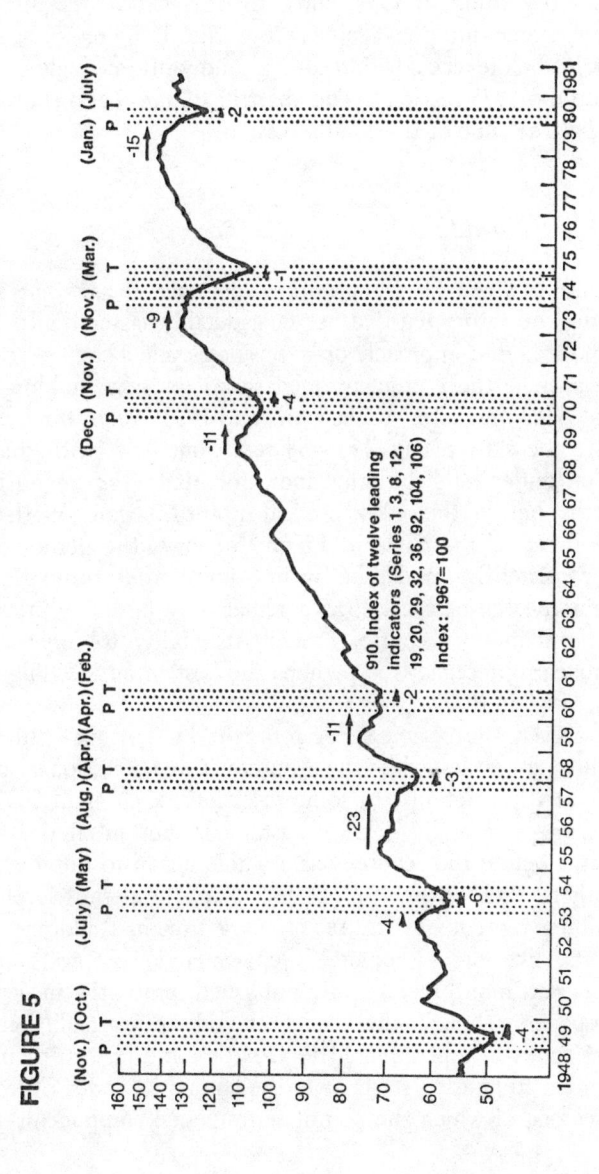

910. Index of twelve leading indicators (Series 1, 3, 8, 12, 19, 20, 29, 32, 36, 92, 104, 106)

Index: 1967=100

covery beginning in 1954, three months before the 1958 recovery, three months again before the 1961 recovery, four months before the 1970 recovery, and only a single month before the 1975 recovery. The chart in Figure 5 also shows the leads at the time of the 1980 recession.

Building Permits

Within this general framework, experience shows that some leading indicators tend to act considerably faster than others in spotting the approach of a business-cycle peak or trough. One such is the aforementioned series for new building permits. This indicator peaked in mid-1950, fully three years before the start of the 1953–54 recession. And, with that recession under way, the same indicator hit bottom a full eight months before the 1954 cyclical upturn began. With rare exceptions, as the chart in Figure 6 shows, the permit series has consistently served, in turning point after turning point within the business cycle, as a remarkably farseeing precursor of the economy's course. Indeed, its ability to forewarn of approaching recessions is perhaps the best of any leading indicator listed in *BCD*.

However, the permit series foresight in spotting upturns in the business cycle—while the economy is in a recessionary phase—appears less notable. In some recessions, such as in 1953–54, building permits did begin a sustained, substantial rise many months before the economy as a whole began to improve. But in others, such as the 1973–75 recession, the permit level kept declining right up to the recessionary trough. Building-permit reports, like the Commerce Department's composite index, come out monthly and are published promptly in leading newspapers, though the reader should be warned that the series receives surprisingly little attention and far less than that accorded to housing starts or to the composite index of leading indicators, of which the permit series is one component.

KEEPING AHEAD OF THE CYCLE

FIGURE 6

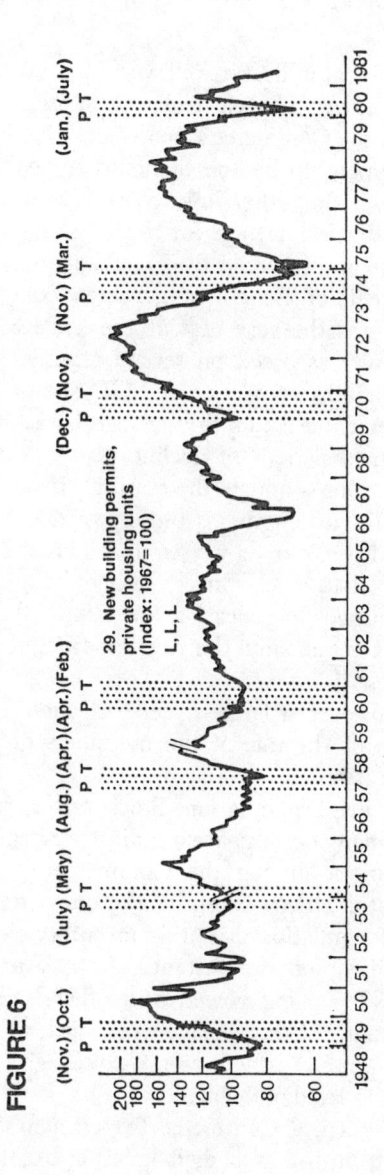

29. New building permits, private housing units (Index: 1967=100) L, L, L

Stock-Price Index

Another individual indicator well worth monitoring extraclosely is the stock market. The particular stock-price index used as a component in the Commerce Department's composite of twelve indicators happens to be the Standard & Poor's index of 500 common stocks. But other indexes, such as the more famous Dow Jones industrial average for thirty leading stocks, also can serve as leading indicators of the broad economy. As noted, the National Bureau of Economic Research concluded that the stock market was the very best of the key leading indicators. The assessment was based on several criteria, including timeliness and reliability. A glance at BCD shows that the stock-price index, used on a monthly-average basis, has consistently entered sustained periods of decline many months before the onset of recessions—though the warning times have not generally been quite as lengthy as those provided by the building-permit series. Moreover, as we see in the chart in Figure 7, the record shows that stock prices, like building permits, have consistently turned up at least a few months before recoveries have started. Occasionally, the lead time before a recovery has been extensive.

There is, however, a large caveat that should be inserted in any discussion of the role of the usefulness of stock prices as a leading indicator.

The caveat involves inflation. Stock prices, for all their excellence over many decades as an indicator of coming economic trends, are unique among the Commerce Department's key leading indicators. They comprise the only one of the twelve *not* adjusted for inflation. Monthly inventory changes and new consumer-goods orders, for instance, are measured in terms of the dollar's 1972 buying power. Still other leading indicators, such as the length of the average work week or the number of new building permits issued, aren't expressed in terms of any sort of dollars, inflated or deflated.

Brian D. Kajutti, a Commerce Department economist, has explained that, until double-digit inflation began in the 1970s,

KEEPING AHEAD OF THE CYCLE

FIGURE 7

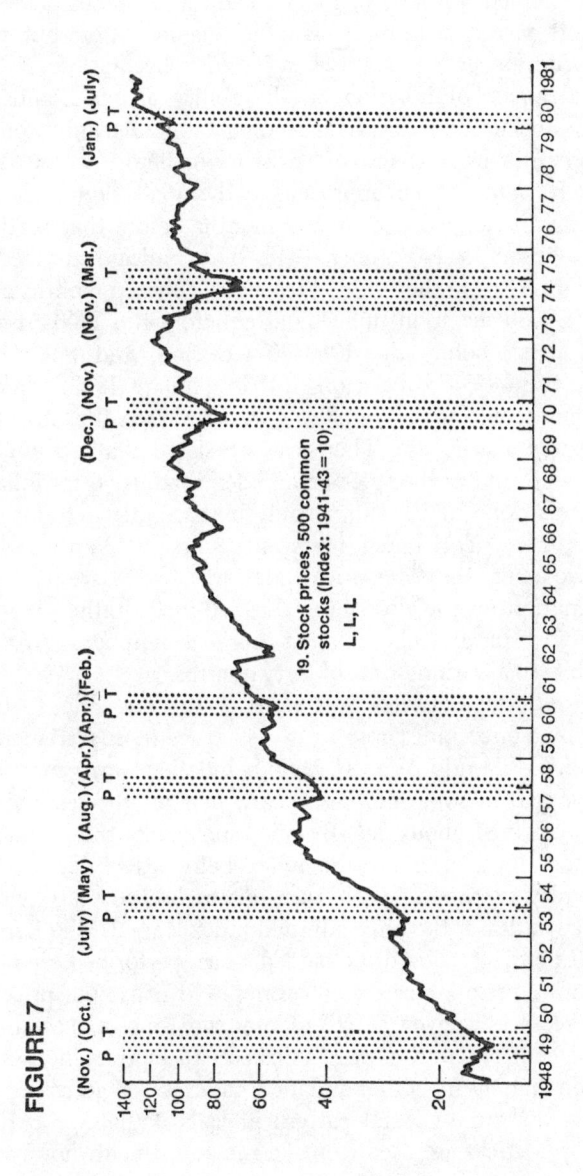

19. Stock prices, 500 common stocks (Index: 1941-43 = 10)
L, L, L

"there seemed no need to inflation-adjust the stock-price indicator. It served beautifully as a leading indicator, but that's clearly no longer the case" when inflation becomes severe.

The impact of inflation on the ability of the Standard & Poor's stock-price index, as a leading economic indicator, can be seen in a brief review of its behavior before various recessions. It signaled the approach of the 1948–49 recession by entering a sustained decline five months before that particular slump began in November 1948. The indicator flashed red six months before the 1953–54 recession, thirteen months before the 1957–58 recession, nine months before the 1960–61 recession, a year before the 1969–70 recession, and ten months before the 1973–75 recession. But in January 1980, when the economy once again entered a down-phase, the stock-price index was on the rise. There was no signal that a slump was imminent—unless the stock-price index is adjusted for inflation. This was done in 1980 in a study by Sanford C. Bernstein & Co., a New York-based investment adviser. With inflation squeezed out, the stock-price index was by no stretch of the imagination on the rise at the start of 1980. Rather, it was in the midst of a decline dating from September 1976. That amounts to a warning time of forty months.

A *footnote*: Between September 1976 and early 1980, the consumer price index rose nearly 40 percent. In earlier phases of the post-World War II period, inflation was generally far less severe. In some of those years, in fact, the general price level remained about flat. By no coincidence, the recessionary warning times given by the index before the previous recessions, dating back to 1948, turn out to be the same, whether the raw index or the price-adjusted index is used. The Bernstein adjustment, it should be added, was performed employing consumer price increases. For example, if consumer prices rose 10 percent in a given length of time and stock prices also rose 10 percent, then the price-adjusted stock-price index would remain flat. Using other inflation indexes for adjusting stock prices, the same general pattern prevails. Whatever particular price yardsticks are used to make the adjustment, however, the point to remember is that in times of high inflation stock prices serve as good leading indicators only when adjusted to take inflation out of the picture. Unfortunately, an inflation-adjusted stock-price index isn't readily available, but to make the adjustment yourself is simple. As indicated above, just match the percentage rise in prices each month against the percentage stock-price increase. Two 10 percent gains, for example, would mean no change for the month in "real" stock prices.

Usually, of course, the respective gains (or reductions) won't exactly match one another. Let's suppose that in a given month the consumer price index rises at an annual rate of 12 percent (consumer price changes are carried in *The Wall Street Journal* and other major newspapers on the day after the Bureau of Labor Statistics issues its monthly press release covering the index). Let's further suppose in the particular month that the Standard & Poor's index of 500 common stocks rises from 110 to 114; using a pocket calculator (or simply long division), you readily see that this works out to gain of about 3.6 percent. To annualize this, you then merely multiply by 12 (since there are twelve months in a year). You come up with an annualized stock-price rise for the month of about 43 percent. (We won't bother figuring in the effects of compounding, since it's a complicated procedure and won't make a significant difference in the result that you're after.) Now you simply subtract 12 percent from 43 percent and so determine that in "real" terms the share-price indicator rose in the month in question at an annual rate of approximately 31 percent.

The Money Supply

A third key leading indicator that seems well worth keeping tabs on is the money supply, again adjusted to eliminate growth due merely to inflation. All sorts of money-supply data are issued on a weekly basis by the Federal Reserve Board in Washington. They carry various "M" labels—M1, M2, M3, and so on. It is too much to expect the average investor to define and attempt to follow all these weekly Fed reports, which in any event are stated in what economists call "nominal" terms —that is, unadjusted for inflation. But investors can and should try to keep tabs on the inflation-adjusted money supply on a monthly basis, and this can be accomplished simply by following the numbers as they appear in BCD. The particular "M" shown in the BCD chart in Figure 8—M2—may be defined as demand deposits plus currency in circulation plus most time deposits at commercial banks plus noninstitutional money-market fund holdings.

This money-supply indicator, like stock prices and building permits, has proved an especially reliable precursor of the economy's cyclical ups and downs. Consider, for example, its behavior before and during the 1969–70 recession. That recession began in December 1969 and hit bottom in November 1970. The money-supply indicator, in turn, reached a peak in January 1969, a full eleven months before the business-cycle peak, and hit bottom in February 1970, nine months before the business-cycle trough. Clearly, any investor wise enough to have been monitoring this indicator in those years would have seen the 1969–70 recession coming well ahead of time and also have been in a position to anticipate the economic recovery that began in 1970 long before it was under way.

An astute investor, we should add, would also have noticed that the building-permits series and the Standard & Poor's stock-price index were also on the decline in the early weeks of 1969. By the same token, this investor would have observed that stock prices were once again rising by July of 1970 and that permits had been on the increase since even earlier that year.

It surely would be risky to assume that a recession is approaching or will soon end simply because a single leading indicator points up or down, as the case may be. But when three highly reliable indicators all flash the same message— as happened, for instance, in 1969–70—an even riskier investment course is to go along as though the current economic trend will persist far into the future.

FIGURE 8

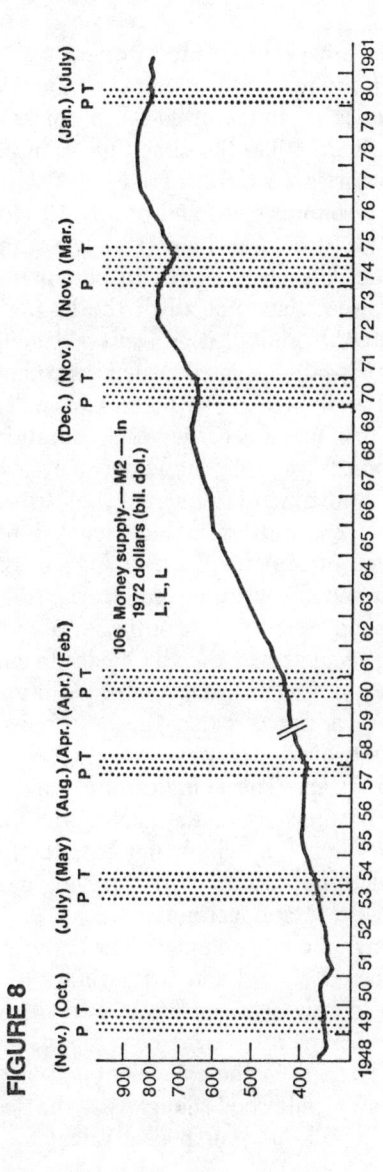

106. Money supply — M2 — In 1972 dollars (bil. dol.)
L, L, L

The Ratio

I've left my favorite leading indicator for last. It's actually a ratio devised from two other Commerce Department indexes. The numerator is an index of so-called coincident indicators, which usually rise or fall at the same time as business in general. The denominator is an index of lagging indicators that normally trail the economy's ups and downs. Economists at Goldman, Sachs & Co., a large New York-based investment concern, adjust the data each month to eliminate any distortion caused by inflation, since not all of the lagging indicators are inflation-adjusted. I think of it as a sort of leading-leading indicator that has repeatedly signaled major turning points in the business cycle well before the better-known leading-indicator index. Like that index, it is carried each month in BCD. While the leading indicators have warned of approaching recessions by an average lead time of about ten months during the post-World War II era, this ratio has signaled recession by an average of some fifteen months. For instance, as seen in the chart in Figure 9, the warning before the 1973–75 recession given by the ratio was eleven months, or about twice as long as the warning given at that time by the leading-indicator index.

An explanation for this remarkable ability to foreshadow slumps so far in advance is that the ratio reflects how swiftly in relation to overall economic activity the various lagging indicators are rising. These indicators, remember, represent facets of the business scene that act to inhibit further economic growth when they climb much faster than the broad-gauged coincident indicators. Typical lagging indicators include the bank prime rate and per-unit labor costs. Typical coincident indicators include employment and the industrial-production index. I should add that, while the ratio is carried in BCD each month, you can easily work it out for yourself from monthly Commerce Department reports, carried in newspapers, of the changes in the coincident and lagging indicators. These are usually published along with the leading-indicator changes. Simply pull out your pocket calculator and make the

KEEPING AHEAD OF THE CYCLE 101

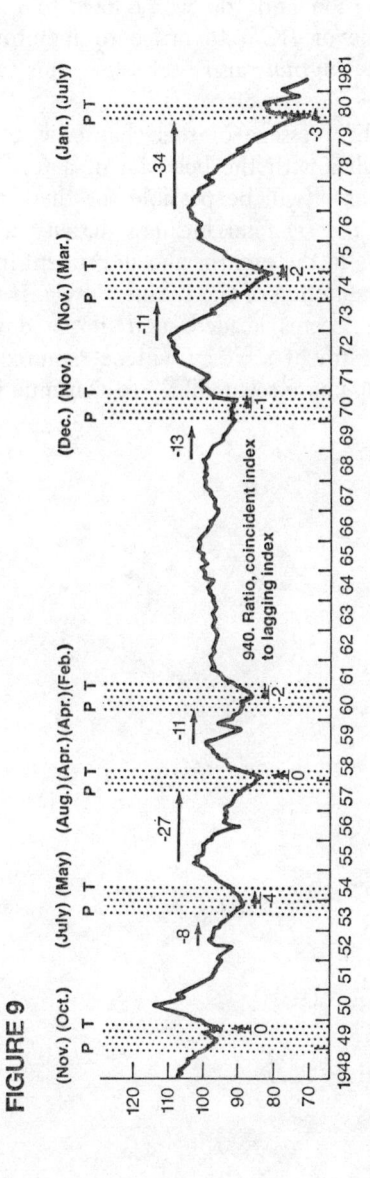

FIGURE 9

necessary division and you won't have to wait for your next monthly issue of *BCD* to arrive to monitor the ratio. *The Wall Street Journal* also publishes this calculation every month.

In sum, the message of this chapter is to urge readers to become familiar with the behavior of a few key leading indicators, so that it will be possible for them to detect well in advance whether general business activity will be expanding or contracting in the months ahead. Prudent investing demands a clear understanding of the business cycle. If the cycle is in an up-phase, but seems headed soon into a down-phase, a very different investment strategy will be required than if, for example, the up-phase seems likely to continue indefinitely.

10.
Riding the Stock Market

DURING THE SUMMER OF 1976 I RECEIVED A BRIEF NOTE FROM A *Wall Street Journal* reader named Sanford D. Hecht, a Waltham, Massachusetts, ophthalmologist. He kindly wrote to say that he had enjoyed various *Journal* articles over the years. He went on: "Also, I wondered if you could recommend some basic reports which are simply stated, so that I would find them useful in making decisions for myself. I have been so badly burned and disappointed with experts in the advisory services that I have decided to use my own—which in the past has been better—judgment. . . . Can you help?"

The advice that I offered in response to the doctor's appeal was the same simple counsel that has been offered thus far in this book: Watch the business cycle, watch it yourself, and invest accordingly. But another question arises—invest in what?

There are many investment vehicles available to those with the wherewithal—stocks, bonds, short-term money market bills and notes, tangibles ranging from soybeans to gold, and real estate.

A premise of this book is that investing for yourself can be —and should be—kept simple. There are probably all sorts of other demands on your time, including probably a full-time job. So don't become overly concerned about esoteric investment techniques that would require enormous amounts of your attention. Later we will run through a list of "don'ts," a sampling of the highly complicated investment arrangements that aren't normally for do-it-yourselfers.

Keep It Simple

By keeping things simple, I mean that you shouldn't try, for instance, to follow hundreds of different stocks listed on the various securities exchanges around the country. Nor should you attempt to monitor the scores of economic statistics listed, for example, in *BCD*. A sensible investment technique would be to pick out a half dozen or so leading industries and focus, say, on several major companies in each industry. Obvious industry choices would include auto making, other consumer-goods production, retailing, homebuilding, capital equipment, and public utilities.

By the same token, stick with the indicators stressed in the previous chapter—the composite leading-indicator index, such farseeing precursors as building permits, the stock market as reflected in the Standard & Poor's index of 500 common stocks, the inflation-adjusted money supply, the ratio of coincident to lagging indicators.

Keeping things simple still permits a wide enough selection of investment vehicles. Always bear in mind the crucial importance of the business cycle. Perhaps the most obvious place to invest, and one often offering great potential gain, is the stock market. It certainly receives the lion's share of publicity in the financial press. When you buy shares of stock, of course, you become a part owner of the particular corporation. Normally, you will receive a quarterly dividend payment on your shares. The precise amount of the payment will depend on such factors as the state of the company's earnings and the outlook as gauged by the board of directors.

The stock of major companies—the ones that would represent leaders in their respective industries—generally are listed on the New York Stock Exchange, or "Big Board," as stockbrokers call it, in downtown Manhattan. There is also the American Stock Exchange, located a few blocks north and west of the New York Stock Exchange. Smaller regional exchanges exist in such cities as Boston, Philadelphia, and San Francisco. When you buy stock on any of these exchanges, you normally will be purchasing the stock through a stockbroker from an existing stockholder willing to sell. Accordingly, the money that you pay doesn't go to the company in question. The rare exception would be when you buy a new issue of stock. This would involve newly issued stock of a company attempting to raise funds through so-called equity financing. In such transactions, one or more investment-banking firms usually will buy the new stock directly from the issuing corporation and then resell it as a new issue to public investors. Such new stock generally is handled on the "over-the-counter" stock market, rather than on the more formal, more strictly regulated stock exchanges mentioned above. Eventually, such OTC stock may wind up, say, on the Big Board, but only after the corporation has applied to "list" them there and met various "listing" requirements aimed at safeguarding investors.

How does the stock market in general behave with regard to the business cycle? How does this general pattern vary from industry to industry? When should other considerations, besides the business cycle itself, also be taken into account?

A Closer Look

We have seen, very briefly, that a distinct relationship exists between stock-price movements and the business cycle. Now, let's take a closer, more practical look, at that relationship. The table "Stock Prices and Business Cycles" traces the link between stocks and the ups and downs of business through the first three quarters of this century.

Stock Prices and Business Cycles

BUSINESS CYCLE PEAK	BUSINESS CYCLE TROUGH	MONTHS FROM STOCK MARKET HIGH TO BUSINESS PEAK	MONTHS FROM BUSINESS PEAK TO MARKET LOW	MONTHS FROM STOCK MARKET LOW TO BUSINESS TROUGH
Sept. 1902	Aug. 1904	5	14	9
May 1907	June 1908	16	6	7
Jan. 1910	Jan. 1912	3	6	18
Jan. 1913	Dec. 1914	4	23	0
Aug. 1918	Mar. 1919	21	−8	15
Jan. 1920	July 1921	2	19	−1
May 1923	July 1924	2	5	9
Oct. 1926	Nov. 1927	2	3	10
Aug. 1929	Mar. 1933	−1	35	8
May 1937	June 1938	2	10	3
Nov. 1948	Oct. 1949	5	7	4
July 1953	May 1954	6	2	8
Aug. 1957	Apr. 1958	16	2	6
Apr. 1960	Feb. 1961	4	6	4
Dec. 1969	Nov. 1970	12	5	6
Nov. 1973	Mar. 1975	10	13	3

This table happens to be based on the Dow Jones industrial average of thirty leading stocks. The leads and lags, however, would be very nearly the same for the Standard & Poor's index of 500 stocks. The peaks and troughs of the business cycle are based on findings of the National Bureau of Economic Research, the Cambridge, Massachusetts, arbiter in such business-cycle matters.

Even a cursory glance at the table turns up useful hints for the do-it-yourself investor. In the sixteen sequences, we see, for example, that stock prices reached a high before the business cycle reached a high no less than fifteen times, and often by many months—sixteen months in 1907–8, twenty-one months in 1918–19, and sixteen months in 1957–58. Only once, on the other hand, did the business peak precede the stock market peak. This was in 1929–33, the onset of the Great Depression, and the lag was only a single month. One theory is that the violence of the October 1929 crash in stock prices was such that it actually contributed to—rather than merely reflected the approach of—a severe retrenchment in overall economic activity. Until the market crashed, the slowdown in the economy had been relatively mild.

In any event, the general message is clear: The stock market will be on the way down by the time business generally begins to take a tumble. In other words, don't wait until the economy has reached a business-cycle peak before getting out of the stock market. The time to exit is several months earlier, at the least.

Another cursory glance makes clear that stock prices almost always—the exception is the 1918–19 recession—hit bottom many months after the economy begins to nose-dive. Much of the time, we see, the period involved has ranged in the area of five to seven months. But occasionally the lag has been much longer.

Regardless, the lesson to be learned is this: Just as you don't want to wait until a recession is actually under way before bailing out of the stock market, you also don't want to be in too much of a hurry to buy back into the stock market, once it's apparent that business really is in a slump. However, don't, by any means, wait until a recession is over to get back into the market.

This brings us to the final column of the table, which shows the time elapsed between the stock market's low point and the subsequent low point in the economy. Again, only once has a recession ended before the stock market has turned up again. In the fifteen other episodes shown, the stock market was on the rise for never less than three months, and, more often, for a good deal longer. Twice the lead time exceeded one year.

The message here is vital to prudent stock-market investing. To repeat: Don't wait until the economy is recovering to get back into the stock market. If you do, you will miss a golden investment opportunity to buy stocks cheaply. Moreover, as we will see, the sharpest stock-price increases often occur in this period, shortly before the end of a recession, precisely when the general economic news seems black and establishment figures are proclaiming that there is absolutely no glimmer of light at the end of the business tunnel. If you're watching the various indicators discussed earlier in this book, you'll be several giant steps ahead of the game.

Here's one brief illustration of how an awareness of the relationship between the business cycle and stock prices could have paid off. December 8, 1969, was a gloomy time for many stockholders. The Dow Jones industrial stock average was 785.04, steeply below its mid-May reading of approximately 970. Moreover, the economy seemed headed into a recession. Company earnings were dropping. It hardly seemed a time for optimism about stock-market prospects. An investor keeping tabs on the various key precursors discussed earlier would have seen that the onset of a recession was imminent, and he would have further appreciated that an opportune time to buy stocks probably lay down the road a few months.

The record shows that, predictably, the Dow Jones average hit a bottom of 631.16 in May of 1970, five months after the recession's start. But then consider the stock-price pattern. By April of 1971 a stock-market explosion had occurred. In that month, six months into the economy's recovery from the trough of the 1969–70 recession, the Dow Jones industrial average stood at 950.82, a precipitous climb of nearly 320 points on the Dow in less than a year. And it was a turnaround that a close student of the economic indicators mentioned earlier could reasonably have foreseen. He or she would have seen the coming turnaround clearly foreshadowed in the various leading indicators that we've said should be monitored on a regular basis. For instance, the student of the market would have noted that by the spring of 1970 the aforementioned building-permits series was in a sustained upturn.

Timing Is Vital

The importance of timing—when to pull out of the stock market, when to move in—can hardly be overstated. The reason, in large measure, is that the market's turns tend to be exceedingly sharp. For instance, the Dow Jones industrial stock average reached a low of 577.60 in December 1974, three months before the pit of the 1973–75 recession. In mid-April 1975, with the recession at last plainly over, the same stock-price index stood at 819.46, a 42 percent rise from the December nadir. Nothing like that gain lay ahead, as the new up-phase of the business cycle continued and broadened. Indeed, when the long up-phase finally ended in January 1980, nearly five years later, the Dow Jones average was in the mid-800 range, barely higher than all the way back in April 1975. At some points in between, it should be added, the index was substantially lower than in April 1975. For example, it dipped as low as 742.12 in early 1978, a year of continuing economic growth.

Timing is equally vital in any decision to pull out of the market when the indicators show that a recession is brewing.

A huge fraction of the recessionary drop in stock prices will have already occurred if you wait until a recession is actually under way. For instance, the 1973–75 recession began in November 1973, while the Dow Jones average reached its high for the preceding up-phase of the business cycle—at 1051.70—a full ten months earlier. By the time the recession was actually under way, the stock-price index was in the low-800 range. Thus, an investor who waited until the recession arrived to pull out of the market would have sustained a loss on the Dow Jones average of roughly 250 points, or slightly more than the further fall of this index to its recessionary low in December 1974.

To be sure, the time lapsing between the broad ups and downs of the stock market and those of the economy as a whole varies from one episode in the business cycle to the next. But in the main, the rule is that the time to get out of stocks is well before a recession begins, and the time to get into stocks is well before a recession ends. And, of course, your guides to both maneuvers are the various indicators discussed earlier.

A large warning, however, must be recalled. The stock market's relationship with the business cycle can be seriously distorted by high, persistent levels of inflation. When the economy lapsed into still another down-phase of the business cycle in January 1980, the broad stock-price index issued for 500 common stocks by Standard & Poor's averaged 110.87, on a base of 1941–43=10. This was up from 107.78 in December 1979 and from 103.66 in November 1979. It far exceeded the level a year earlier of 99.71. It was higher, in fact, than any monthly Standard & Poor's reading since early 1973. The index rose further to 115.34 in February 1980, the first full month of the new recession. The June 1980 reading, with the recession a half-year old, was 114.55, some four points higher than when the slump began in January.

Where, in that record, appears the warning of a recession's approach? As noted, the Standard & Poor's stock-price index is among the key indicators that economists follow for early glimpses of the business road ahead. Where, moreover, is that traditional linkage between stock prices and the business cycle?

Nowhere—unless inflation can be squeezed out of the stock-price picture.

This can be readily done. Using as the inflation adjustment vehicle the Commerce Department's index for personal consumption expenditures—a broad and exceedingly accurate inflation gauge—we find that stock-price behavior was really quite normal as the 1980 recession neared. The stock-market peak preceding the recession, as noted, turned out to be September 1976, a remarkably long lead time of plus forty months, instead of minus one month. In February 1980, when the unadjusted index hit a peak of 115.34, the inflation-free version was at 66.33, some 16 percent under its level in September 1976. Over the same interval, in contrast, the unadjusted index rose about 10 percent.

These dichotomous patterns coincided with a period of extraordinary inflation. Between September 1976 and February 1980 consumer prices rose, on the average, about 40 percent.

In sum, the relationship between stock-price trends and the ups and downs of the business cycle has long served as a guide to prudent investors as well as to economic forecasters wise enough to monitor such precursors. Generally, the best time to plunge into stocks has been around the middle of a recession, and the best time to get out of the market has been a year or more before the onset of a recession. However, to repeat, beware of inflation. An investor using this strategy in, say, February 1979, when most leading indicators other than the stock market were already flashing red, would have bailed out unnecessarily.

A *footnote*: If a person owned $1,051.70 worth of stocks in the Dow Jones average in January 1973, when the index peaked, it would have required $2,074.58 worth of the Dow Jones average in November 1980 to buy the same amount of goods and services that the $1,051.70 could buy in January 1973. (By "owning" the average, we mean that an investor would divide money among the thirty industrial stocks that make up the Dow Jones index. The list changes from time to time. In late 1981, for example, the thirty stocks used were Allied Corp.; Aluminum Co. of America; American Brands; American Can; American Telephone & Telegraph; Bethlehem Steel; Du Pont;

Eastman Kodak; Exxon; General Electric; General Foods; General Motors; Goodyear; Inco; IBM; International Harvester; International Paper; Johns-Manville; Merck; Minnesota Mining & Manufacturing; Owens-Illinois; Procter & Gamble; Sears, Roebuck; Standard Oil of California; Texaco; Union Carbide; United Technologies; U. S. Steel; Westinghouse Electric; and Woolworth.)

The stock market, of course, includes a multitude of businesses and, within those businesses, a huge number of individual companies. Armed with an understanding of how the stock market as a whole behaves in relationship to the business cycle, let us now inspect precisely how particular categories of stocks relate to the economy's broad ups and downs.

11.
Picking Stocks

THE STOCK MARKET'S GENERAL BEHAVIOR, WE HAVE SEEN, RESPONDS in a predictable fashion to the ups and downs of the business cycle. The pattern can be roughly anticipated by any investor who takes the trouble to assess, by use of the key indicators, the economy's near-term course. It's also possible, employing similar tactics, to anticipate prospective movements of individual types of stocks within the broad market's general trend. Again, the crucial exercise is to try to relate a particular type of stock first to the behavior of the market as a whole and then to the business cycle.

Consider, for example, a company involved in the production of machine tools. Let's call it the XYZ Widget Company. The nub is that XYZ Widget produces machine tools, which account for a sizable amount of business spending for new plant and equipment. A perusal of *Business Conditions Digest* will quickly tell you that plant-and-equipment outlays behave as a lagging indicator. Such expenditures tend to hit their highs for a cycle somewhat after the economy as a whole peaks before heading into a broad recession. And they tend to reach low points somewhat later than when the economy hits bottom.

In other words, such spending is apt to keep dropping for a while, even though business activity in general has turned around from a recession and is on the recovery road. In the severe 1973–75 recession, for instance, plant-and-equipment spending peaked in late 1974, almost a year after that slump began. And the expenditure figure didn't hit a low until near the end of 1975, even though the economy as a whole began recovering as early as March of 1975.

The investing lesson to draw from this is that the ups and downs of machine-tool stocks—like those of XYZ Widget—will tend to lag behind the ups and downs of the stock market generally. When the economy is approaching a business-cycle peak, XYZ Widget stock will tend to hold up longer than most stocks. And when most stocks begin rising again with the approach of the recovery, XYZ Widget stock will tend to stay depressed longer.

This tendency is apparent, among other places, in a "relative strength" index for machinery producers prepared by the Value Line Investment Survey. This index, using June 1967 as a base, compares the average stock-price level for machinery concerns with a broad Value Line composite average for stocks generally. In effect, it's a ratio of machinery-industry stock prices to the general stock-price level. In early 1973, with the 1973–75 recession still some eleven months off, the ratio stood just above 140. By the start of 1974, however, with the recession a couple of months under way, the same index was up to about 220. In other words, machinery stock prices, reflecting the industry's habitual "lag" in the business cycle, were holding up well as the recession began, while the market generally was on the decline. By the same token, in early 1975, when the recession was ending, the ratio fell substantially, to about the 180 level. And it remained well under the 200-plus range of early 1974 for about another year. By then, a new up-phase of the business cycle had been rolling for more than a year. The upshot is that, generally speaking, machinery stock should be among the last to jump back into when a recovery is beginning to take shape on the horizon.

In any such investment decisions, of course, long-term considerations should be taken into account, along with business-cycle factors. Because of competition from abroad and tax regulations over many years tending to discourage investment in new plant and equipment, a case can be made that machinery stocks were not worth buying at any time in recent decades. That's a decision that one must ponder carefully. Import restrictions, as well as tax rules, can change from year to year. The point to remember here is that, if you are invested in any such securities, or wish to be, a familiarity with their very special relationship to the business cycle will keep you several large steps ahead of the game. The reasons for the machine-tool industry's tendency to lag behind the business cycle are complex. They include, for instance, the fact that business planners are usually slow to foresee major turning points in the economy's direction. But the record over many decades leaves no question about the tendency, and the investor who is aware of it is obviously at a large advantage.

The machine-tool industry is by no means alone in its special behavior vis-à-vis the business cycle.

Playing Housing

Readers will recall that building permits and, to a lesser degree, new-home starts are among the *BCD*'s leading indicators of general economic activity. That is to say, the home-building industry tends to move into a slump somewhat sooner than business generally and also to pull out somewhat sooner. Occasionally, business-cycle history makes clear, this lead time has been pronounced. For instance, home starts peaked a full year before the onset of the 1969–70 recession and began rising again when that eleven-month recession was barely under way. More typical was the pattern evident in 1960–61. The level of home starts peaked within six months of the onset of the 1960–61 recession and hit bottom a full quarter before the recession itself hit bottom.

The lesson here for investors is that stocks tied largely to home building will tend to decline somewhat sooner before a recession than the market as a whole and to rise somewhat sooner than the market generally before a recovery begins. Indeed, the pattern is the opposite of that described earlier for machinery shares. The Value Line Investment Survey, again, has tracked the "relative strength" of building-industry shares over the years. Not surprisingly, it shows that, relative to stocks generally, this stock group began losing strength a particularly long while before the onset of the 1973–75 recession and, by the same token, began rising in the fall of 1974, several months before the market as a whole hit bottom (which in turn, we should note, preceded by several months the March 1975 bottom of the recession itself). A similar relationship of building shares to the stock market generally is apparently at other business-cycle turning points.

Consumer-stock Behavior

Just as home-building activity tends to be a leading indicator and machine-tool business a lagging indicator, consumer spending invariably behaves, in the jargon of economists, as a "coincident" indicator. It moves up or down coincidentally with the economy as a whole. It generally peaks when the economy is turning from an expansionary phase of the business cycle into a recessionary phase, and it usually reaches a trough when the economy is moving from a recession into a recovery.

With this in mind, an investor can safely—and correctly—presume that stocks closely tied to the consumer will tend to move up or down at approximately the same time as the stock market in general. This pattern is readily apparent, for example, among stocks of companies engaged in the manufacture of apparel, a business dominated by consumer tastes. The Value Line relative-strength index for this industry shows this tendency. For instance, it remained virtually flat through nearly the entire 1973–75 recession. In mid-1975, with the recession over, it stood at precisely the level recorded in the fall of 1973, just before the recession began.

A similar pattern is evident among stocks representing firms engaged in the retail-store business. These stocks tend to decline and then recover approximately in unison with the market's general trend. Like the apparel group, the relative strength of the retailer shares after the 1973–75 recession, at slightly over the 100 mark, about matched the prerecessionary reading.

Consumer-related industries aren't the only ones that fall under the broad category of coincident economic indicators. Important areas of manufacturing, for example, tend to move up or down concurrently with the world economy. *Business Conditions Digest* doesn't precisely classify each industry— leading, coincident, or lagging—in terms of its business-cycle relationship. However, an inspection of the *BCD's* various charts, which as we have observed run through up- and downphases of the business cycle, provides a clear enough indication of how different manufacturing enterprises tend to perform. And this, in turn, provides the timing clue that an investor will need in keying buy or sell decisions to the business cycle.

A review of *BCD* shows, for example, that spending for cars tends to move coincidentally with the business cycle. Accordingly, it's no surprise to find that auto stocks have generally moved in tandem with the general market. It should also be pointed out, however, that an important distinction is apparent between the auto-making business and truck manufacturing. Autos are clearly consumer-related and, as such, a coincident indicator of the economy. Trucks, on the other hand, are normally a capital investment and, as such, a component of the broad plant-and-equipment category, which as we have seen, tends to lag behind the ups and downs of the business cycle. In this regard, it's significant that trucking stocks, relative to auto stocks, gained strength sharply in the early stages of the 1973–75 recession and then lost ground to auto stocks around the end of that recession.

The behavior of auto stocks also provides a reminder that the prudent do-it-yourself investor cannot afford to focus exclusively on business-cycle relationships. This danger is apparent, for instance, in the auto-stock performance during 1973–75. That recession, of course, encompassed the first big Arab oil squeeze, a now-familiar development that obviously hit the auto industry particularly hard. Accordingly, it's no surprise that the relative strength of auto stocks, which gained somewhat as the recession ended, nonetheless remained appreciably below prerecessionary levels. As late as mid-1976, the strength reading for auto stocks was below 90, on a base of 1967=100. That is, the mid-1976 reading amounted to 90 percent of the 1967 average. In mid-1973, several months before the 1973–75 recession and before the beginning of the Arab oil squeeze, the auto strength reading was close to 110.

Shares of stock in particular industries, we see, respond in particular ways to the ups and downs of the business cycle. Housing stocks tend to lead the cycle, as well as the market in general. Auto stocks normally behave in a coincidental manner. The machine-tool stocks tend to lag.

Most businesses, by and large, exhibit similar sorts of relationships. The home-appliance industry, for example, generally behaves as a coincidental indicator. At first glance, one might suppose that, with its link to home building, the appliance industry would tend to lead the economy and the market. But the fact is that appliance demand generally lags behind home-building activity—for the obvious reason that new homes must be started before they can be equipped with ranges, refrigerators, dishwashers, and so on.

A Long List

The list goes on. It will come as no surprise that the cement industry, to cite another instance, tends to behave as a lagging indicator. It is directly tied to capital spending patterns, which, as noted, distinctly lag behind the economy's cyclical turning points. The tendency is apparent in the Value Line relative-

PICKING STOCKS

strength index for the cement group of stocks. The index, again with 1967 as a base, rose sharply as the 1973–75 recession set in, to more than 140 from about 110 just before the slump's onset. And as the recession ended in the spring of 1975, the index kept dropping, to a low of about 100 at year's end from about 130 early in the year.

It should also come as no surprise that the forest-products group of stocks normally functions as a leading economic indicator. While the cement industry is generally linked to capital spending—new plants, new highways, and the like—the forest-products industry is broadly tied to the housing industry. And that business, as we have observed, falls clearly under the heading of a leading economic indicator. As 1975 progressed and cement shares were a losing group within the broad stock market, it's no coincidence that the strength index for the forest-products group was sharply on the rise—to nearly 250 from just under the 200 mark early in the year.

It's difficult, in fact, to find many industries that aren't in some way linked to the ups and downs of the business cycle. If the do-it-yourself investor comprehends the nature of the business cycle and how various facets of the broad economy fit into the business-cycle picture, a little common sense should provide the insight necessary to assess the exact role of a particular industry group. If you know that the housing industry is a leading economic indicator, it hardly requires genius to deduce that forest-products shares behave in a similar fashion in relation to the business cycle. If you know that plant-and-equipment spending behaves as a lagging indicator, you may safely deduce that firms making cement, with which new plants are built, will also normally behave as a lagging indicator. If you know that consumer spending, on the other hand, performs generally as a coincident indicator, it will hardly surprise you to learn that the countless businesses closely geared to consumer spending will tend to move up or down coincidentally with the economy.

The table "Twenty-nine Industries" lists a wide assortment

of industries and shows you how over the post-World War II years each has behaved (1) with regard to the business cycle—as a leading, coincident, or lagging indicator—and (2) with regard to the stock market as a whole over many years—that secular-trend question that we discussed in Chapter 7. Note that some industries simply cannot be safely categorized according to their business-cycle behavior. Note also that a few display no significant change in their long-term strength relative to the stock market in general.

Twenty-nine Industries

INDUSTRY	BEHAVIOR IN BUSINESS CYCLE	LONG-TERM BEHAVIOR COMPARED TO ALL STOCKS
Air transport	irregular	getting weaker
Auto making	coincident	getting weaker
Auto parts	coincident	getting stronger
Chemicals	lagging	getting weaker
Cosmetics	irregular	getting weaker
Banking	irregular	getting weaker
Appliances	coincident	getting weaker
Drugs	leading	getting weaker
Electrical equipment	lagging	getting stronger
Housing	leading	no change
Hotel-motel	coincident	no change
Electronics	irregular	getting weaker
Forest products	leading	no change
Leisure time	leading	getting stronger
Construction machinery	lagging	getting stronger
Cement	lagging	getting stronger
Insurance	lagging	getting stronger

INDUSTRY	BEHAVIOR IN BUSINESS CYCLE	LONG-TERM BEHAVIOR COMPARED TO ALL STOCKS
Newspapers	leading	getting stronger
Office equipment	lagging	getting weaker
Petroleum	irregular	getting stronger
Broadcasting	irregular	getting stronger
Railroads	irregular	getting stronger
Restaurants	irregular	no change
Retailing	coincident	getting weaker
Steel	irregular	getting weaker
Textiles	coincident	getting weaker
Tires	irregular	getting weaker
Truck making	lagging	getting weaker
Public utilities	leading	getting weaker

More difficult than assessing where an industry fits into the business-cycle picture is the investing problem of determining into what industry a particular company best fits. There's little question that General Motors Corp., for example, is mainly an automobile producer. It manufactures trucks as well, among many other products, and trucks, as we are aware, are part of capital equipment, a lagging indicator. But GM obviously must be viewed, from an investment standpoint, as a stock whose main business—auto making—will fare coincidentally with the economy as a whole. Accordingly, GM stock can be expected to perform generally in a coincidental manner —moving up or down in approximate tandem with the broad stock market.

The problem of fitting a particular stock into a particular industry can be a lot tougher than trying to categorize General Motors. Is General Electric, with its vast consumer-products business, to be viewed as likely to behave in a coincidental manner? Or, should GE, with its extensive machinery-manu-

FIGURE 10

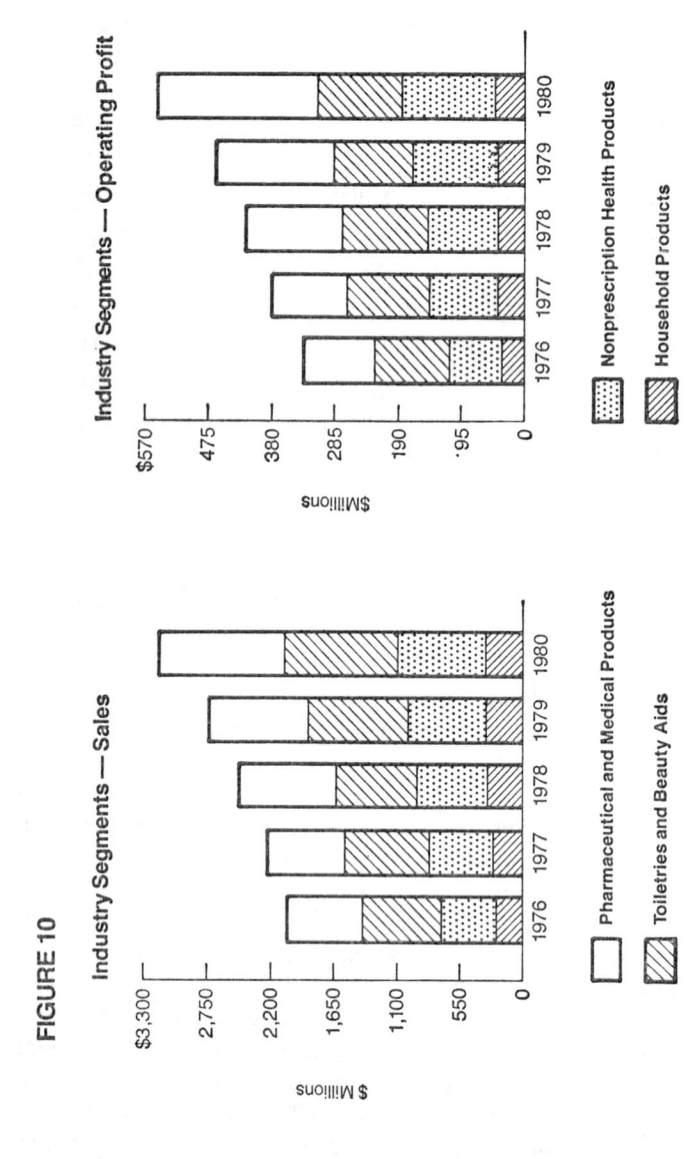

Industry Segments — Sales

Industry Segments — Operating Profit

Pharmaceutical and Medical Products
Nonprescription Health Products
Toiletries and Beauty Aids
Household Products

facturing operation, be viewed as a part of the lagging-indicator sector? How can one possibly categorize a stock like Gulf & Western Industries, whose operations are so diversified that the company's business simply cannot be briefly described?

There are no easy answers to such questions. My suggestion is simply to take a long look at a particular diversified company's situation and determine for yourself what business really constitutes the backbone of its operations. This can usually be done by perusing a recent annual report. These reports normally describe in detail a corporation's activities and place them in perspective. Since annual reports are written for laymen, not for securities analysts on Wall Street, this shouldn't be too difficult a task. And, by taking the trouble, you will be able to see precisely how, within a business-cycle framework, a particular stock should be treated.

Figure 10 is taken from data contained in a recent annual report of Bristol-Myers Co. Is it a consumer-products company? Or a drug company? The breakdown shows that pharmaceutical and other medical products are the largest, fastest-growing part of overall sales and profits. It also makes clear that other consumer items from beauty aids to household products, bulk large in the company's business. Still, you would tend to treat an investment in Bristol-Myers as an investment in the drug industry, which has normally behaved, as the table on page 120 shows, as a leading indicator.

Always keep in mind, whatever stock you decide to buy, that the stock market as a whole behaves as a leading indicator. If you find it difficult to categorize a particular stock in terms of the market as a whole or in terms of the economy, your safest course is to assume that its shares will tend to move up or down in conjunction with the stock market generally. And this, as we spelled out in the previous chapter, means that the time to buy is well before a recession ends, and the time to sell is well before an expansionary phase of the business cycle has run its course.

12.
A
Word
of
Warning

There should be no doubt by now that the investment strategy outlined here places a primary emphasis on linking investment decisions to the ups and downs of the business cycle. Given the nature of the business cycle, such a strategy can neither be characterized as particularly long term or particularly short term in nature. Major business-cycle turning points—down into a recession or up into an economic expansion—don't normally come along every week or month or even year.

The up-phase of the cycle that began in February 1961 went on for more than eight years. Recessions, most happily, tend to be shorter, but they too can hardly be described as brief interludes. The 1973–75 recession lasted nearly a year and a half. Accordingly, by adopting an investment strategy geared to the business cycle, you will adopt a strategy that can best be described, perhaps, as medium term.

You won't have to watch every wiggle of the stock market or every headline that flashes across the business pages every day. But neither can you sit back and forget about your portfolio. Altogether, it's a strategy designed for the interested lay-

A WORD OF WARNING

man, the person who can devote a reasonable amount of time to following events, but not a huge amount.

The strategy of focusing on the business cycle, however, shouldn't blind anyone to the importance of trying to stay reasonably abreast of developments that may go beyond the timing of the economy's cyclical ups and downs. This consideration, as we will see, is particularly important for the stock-market investor.

Most of the larger questions that do-it-yourself investors must ask—the questions that go beyond the business cycle—entail nothing more than a modicum of common sense. To illustrate, let's suppose that you have decided that, from a business-cycle point of view, the time is ripe to buy one hundred shares of a home-building company. You've read in the preceding chapter how best to time such an investment. You know all about the particularly long lead time between the ups and downs of home-building activity, a leading economic indicator, and of the economy as a whole. However, there are several home-building concerns that attract your interest. Which stock to buy? You study their various annual reports and all seem reasonably sound from a financial standpoint. Where should you place your bet?

This is the time to be on the lookout for considerations that may go far beyond the limits of the business cycle. Let's imagine that Home Builder A operates mainly in the Middle Atlantic area, while Home Builder B concentrates his activities in the Southwest. And Home Builder C works the New England area of the country. Now, let's look at a few Commerce Department statistics that trace the behavior of personal income by regions of the country. In the three-year economic up-phase after the 1969–70 recession, personal income rose 32 percent within the United States as a whole, but comparable regional increases ranged far above and below that average. The rise in the Middle Atlantic and New England areas, for example, was only 25 percent, while the comparable Southwest gain was 40 percent.

Moving on, the same pattern is apparent in the period for early 1975 to late 1978, during the general economic upturn from the long 1973–75 recession. For the country in general, personal income climbed 49 percent. But the Middle Atlantic advance was only 37 percent and that for New England only 43 percent. Meanwhile, personal income in the Southwest soared more than 61 percent.

Parenthetically, we should add that the relative strength of the Southwest is also apparent in recessionary phases of the business cycle. During the long 1973–75 slump, personal income in America as a whole rose 12.1 percent, barely keeping pace with inflation. The comparable rise in both the Middle Atlantic area and New England was just 10 percent, while in the Southwest income jumped nearly 17 percent.

Clearly, when the long-term regional factor is taken into account, all other things being equal, the logical investment target is Home Builder B, the company doing business in the relatively robust Southwest region.

Looking Abroad

International as well as national considerations can come into play in this era of globe-girdling corporations. The precise turning points tend to differ from one major industrial country to another. But the record book makes clear that in recent years, ups and downs in the United States business cycle have coincided quite nearly with similar trends in other key economies.

Let's suppose that you plan to invest in XYZ Machine Tool Company, based let us say in Cleveland. The time seems ripe, from a business-cycle perspective, to invest in this company. You are familiar with the tendency of the machine-tool industry to lag behind the economy's ups and downs—to remain relatively strong when many other businesses are beginning to soften and to be soft when the economy generally is starting to regain vigor.

From such a standpoint, you decide that XYZ Machine Tool seems a timely investment buy. But there is another consideration. You have recently noted in the financial pages that the U.S. machine-tool industry, which once was highly competitive in the world marketplace, is beginning to suffer from the difficulty all too familiar in such other industries as steel, auto, and TV manufacturing—competition from abroad, particularly from Japan. So, you must also ask yourself, does the foreign competitive threat to XYZ Machine Tool Company more than offset business-cycle considerations?

You may well decide that the threat from, say, Japanese machine-tool producers is such that it would be best to place your money in some other industry. Or there is another possibility for you. We have noted that economic ups and downs nowadays in different economies tend to coincide. You may decide to stay with the machine-tool industry, but to sink your money into a foreign machine-tool company. Buying into major companies abroad isn't nearly as difficult as you may imagine. Many such corporations are listed on the New York Stock Exchange. Others appear on other U.S. exchanges or can be purchased through most stockbrokers with little extra difficulty or complication. And the effort may well be worth it, for there is little question that stock prices over the long post-World War II pull have fared far better in such major industrial countries as Japan and West Germany than in the United States. In the two decades ending in 1978, the total return to stockholders—capital gains plus dividends plus currency appreciation—averaged about 18 percent yearly in Japan and 14 percent a year in West Germany. The comparable U.S. return to stockholders, based on the performance of the Standard & Poor's index of 500 common stocks, was just over 6 percent.

The charts in Figures 11 and 12 are adapted from an issue of *BCD*. They show, among other things, how very different has been the long-term trend in stock prices from one major country to another. Notice, for instance, how sharply Japanese stock prices have climbed in the dozen years 1969–81, compared with the relative lack of advance in the United States as well as in some other areas.

A WORD OF WARNING

FIGURE 11

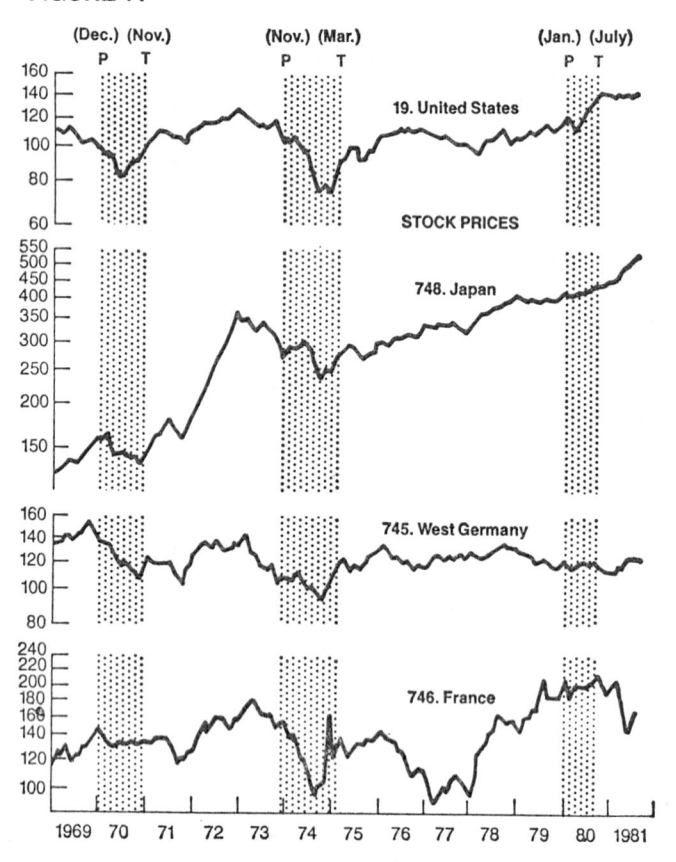

STOCK PRICES

- 19. United States
- 748. Japan
- 745. West Germany
- 746. France

P = Peak, T = Trough
(Dec.) P – (Nov.) T
(Nov.) P – (Mar.) T
(Jan.) P – (July) T

A WORD OF WARNING

FIGURE 12

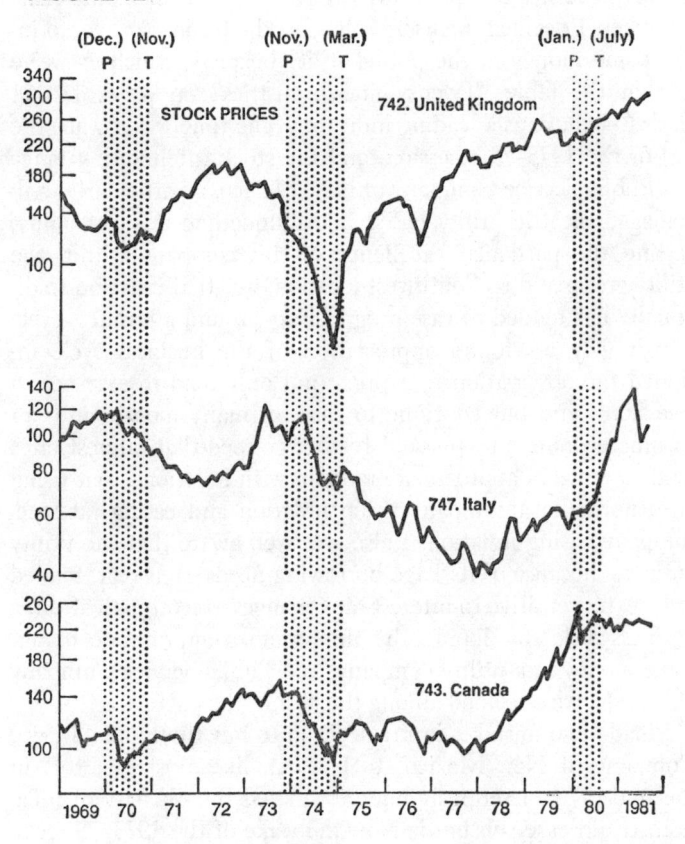

STOCK PRICES
742. United Kingdom
747. Italy
743. Canada

Too Many Shares

Such long-term trends as accelerating inflation, of course, must also be factored into any investment decision, on top of business-cycle developments.

This necessity was painfully driven home for me some years ago when I decided, focusing solely on the business cycle, to invest some money in the public-utility business, which as we've seen in the table "Twenty-nine Industries" on pages 120–21 tends to behave as a leading indicator. The time was toward the end of the 1973–75 recession, and the stock catching my fancy was Public Service Company of New Mexico, a particularly well-managed electric utility based in Albuquerque. My reasoning, beyond the particular excellence of this company within the utility group and its Southwest location, was that inflation traditionally has tended to ease progressively around a business-cycle trough. My newfound appreciation of the business cycle included the observation that prices not only tend to ease near a recession's end but continue to ease for many months into an ensuing economic up-phase. I further grasped that interest rates tend to move in approximate tandem with inflation—that rising rates normally accompany rising inflation and easing rates accompany easing inflation. I also was well aware that the utility business, because of its large borrowing needs each year, tended to be extra sensitive to interest-rate changes. Accordingly, from a business-cycle standpoint, the time seemed appropriate to put some money in a utility company, and Public Service Company of New Mexico seemed among the best of the pack.

I made two mistakes in my decision to buy the Public Service Company of New Mexico stock. First, like most investors in the mid-1970s, I seriously underestimated the tenacity of inflation. It did ease substantially in the wake of the 1973–75 recession, but the reduction proved short-lived. Secondly, I neglected to consider that utility companies, with their large borrowing needs, have another huge avenue open to them when they need funds to keep up their vast facilities. They can issue more common stock, and this is particularly true where the utility in

A WORD OF WARNING

question is deemed especially well-managed and well-positioned geographically. Public Service of New Mexico operates, of course, in the Southwest; the importance of regional considerations was stressed earlier in this chapter.

The company's financial record makes clear the impact of this recurrent issuing of new stock on the value of a single, existing share. In 1975, when I made my small investment in Public Service of New Mexico, its earnings totaled $14.2 million. Five years later, in 1979, they totaled $54.8 million. That's an impressive gain, and one that would suggest a large, concurrent rise in the price per share of Public Service of New Mexico's stock. However, nothing of the sort actually took place. The reason is that in the same five years the average number of shares outstanding more than tripled, to 14,363,000 from 4,609,000. After preferred dividend requirements, net earnings applicable to the company's common stock rose only 52 cents a share, to $2.97. Moreover, the market price per common share at the end of 1979, at $17.27, was actually some $7.00 under the comparable level five years earlier.

A footnote should be appended to the sad investment tale outlined above. It is true that for a brief while after I made the purchase in 1975, the market price of my few Public Service of New Mexico shares rose. The anticipated business-cycle effect as the 1973–75 recession faded into history was such that inflation—and therefore interest rates—did indeed ease dramatically during 1976. It's no coincidence that the utility company's market price per common share at the end of 1976 was $29.95, more than $5.00 above the year-earlier level. What I did not foresee—and, in retrospect, should have foreseen—was the secular nature of inflation in the latter half of the 1970s. Had I been so prescient, I would have understood that, although the developing up-phase of the business cycle still had a long way to go in 1976, the underlying inflationary pressure in the economy was such that inflation—and interest rates—wouldn't stay down for long, and, with the rekindling, there would be a pronounced weakening in the general level of utility-stock prices. This is precisely what happened, of course. Public Service of New

Mexico stock fell to $25.13 at the end of 1977, to $21.31 at the end of 1978, and $17.27 at the end of 1979—and yet there was no interruption in the up-phase of the business cycle from a recession that had ended all the way back in March of 1975.

We see, then, that long-term tendencies within the economy may be neglected at the investor's peril. Common sense should have told me that inflation in those years would persist as a feature of the economic landscape, worsening toward the latter phases of a business-cycle expansion. With the election of President Jimmy Carter in 1976, if not sooner, I should have perceived, but did not, that whatever deflationary benefits may have flowed from the 1973-75 recession had been about exhausted. Such interest-rate sensitive stocks as Public Service of New Mexico should have been plucked from my portfolio. It wasn't, quite simply, because an entirely secular trend—the economy's increasing susceptibility to inflation—had been overlooked. Also neglected had been the logical tactic by which such a well-managed public utility would attempt to minimize its inflation-caused interest costs—through turning whenever possible to new-stock issues.

Politics

The investment importance of factors that go beyond the business cycle extends, of course, to the political arena. We indicated that the best time for selling the Public Service of New Mexico shares would have been just after Jimmy Carter defeated Gerald Ford in the 1976 presidential election. This hardly can be construed as coincidental. Mr. Carter, whatever his virtues as a President may have been, was a naïve observer of the economic scene, and particularly of its latent inflationary pressures. It's beyond dispute that an unfortunate sequence of presidential actions during the early part of his Administration hastened the resurgence of the price spiral that characterized the early part of the decade of the 1980s. But an astute investor might have anticipated this development. Some political understanding would have suggested that this fellow from Plains, Georgia, a Democrat with liberal leanings, would more than likely pursue the sort of policies that would lead to a renewed price spiral. The political factor, in short, should not have been neglected.

In the eighty years from 1900 to 1980, there were forty years when Democratic Presidents were in office and forty Republican years. In those forty Republican years, the Dow Jones industrial average, adjusted for inflation, rose at an annual rate of 1.2 percent. In the forty Democratic years, however, the comparable yearly change in the stock index was *minus* 0.8 percent. The message, unmistakably, is that the stock market tends to perform better when a Republican is in the White House than when a Democrat is. We should add that the picture is very different if no adjustment is made for inflation. Then, the Dow Jones index looks better under the Democrats. It shows a yearly rise of 4.4 percent, against a yearly rise of only 2.1 percent in the forty Republican years. Quite obviously, inflation makes the difference, and inflation was more pronounced in the forty years of Democratic leadership than in the forty Republican years. The precise situation will vary from presidency to presidency, regardless of political party. However, if the do-it-yourself investor wishes to play the odds from a long-term point of view, common-stock investments, stripped of illusory inflationary gains, look a lot better when representatives of the Grand Old Party occupy the White House.

Surging Services

Another development transcending the business cycle is the long-term trend away from manufacturing industries toward the service areas of the economy. Between 1968 and 1978 consumer spending for services rose 175 percent to $620 billion, and the steep climb has persisted since then. By 1980 services employed more than twice as many people as goods-producing industries— 64 million to 30 million. Among the big service job gainers in

1968–78 were health care, up 273 percent; health insurance, up 254 percent; telecommunications, up 181 percent; auto repair, up 233 percent; and utilities such as gas, electricity, and water, up 222 percent. Common sense dictates, in light of such statistics, that investing in a service-industry stock seems likelier over the very long pull to be successful than investing in, say, an industry like steel, where shrinkage rather than growth has been the prevailing pattern. Again, it's a consideration that is long term and goes beyond the business cycle.

At this point, a further word of warning seems appropriate. We have seen in this chapter that in stock-market investing it's always prudent to look beyond the business cycle—although business-cycle considerations should remain at the core of a do-it-yourself investment strategy. We've outlined several of the most important, most obvious of these noncyclical factors—such long-term phenomena as inflation and the swing away from manufacturing to service industries. Be warned that such developments must not be neglected in an overall investment strategy. However, now also be warned that there are distinct limits that the do-it-yourself investor must impose on what to watch and where to look beyond the business cycle. It's prudent to keep any eye on inflation, for example, but don't, as an interested layman, attempt to pursue all sorts of other, highly sophisticated investment tactics as well. You will surely be tempted from time to time to do just that, to spend many hours and possibly much money on learning the intricacies, for instance, of various "technical-analysis" methods of stock-market investing. Leave that to the experts who presumably have the time. Use your time tracking the fundamentals discussed here. Ironically, many expert "technicians" become so absorbed with such esoterica as "double top reversals" and "inverse head and shoulders reversals"—to cite typical technical jargon—that they overlook the forest for the trees. The business cycle and the major secular trends that are readily apparent for all to see, in the process, are forgotten.

I do not mean to suggest that all technical analysis of the stock market is worthless. But I do maintain that such advice can often be dead wrong. Why waste your limited time and energy seeking it? Also, of course, technical stock-market analysis isn't something you can readily do yourself. By leaning on such advice, you no longer are a do-it-yourself investor, and a major argument of this book is that you can and must do it yourself.

Tracking a Technician

What can happen with technical analysis is evident through a long look back at the performance of perhaps the best known and most widely followed of all technical analysts, a man whose sole recommendation in January 1981, for example, was deemed mainly responsible for one of the steepest one-day drops in the long history of the Dow Jones industrial stock average—Joseph E. Granville of Holly Hill, Florida. Mr. Granville is the author of the *Granville Market Letter*, said to have some 16,000 loyal subscribers who recently have been paying at least $250 per year each for the privilege of receiving the distilled wisdom of Mr. Granville's technical analysis.

Let's examine the Granville track record before and during the 1973–75 recession. We've noted that the Dow Jones average, as a leading economic indicator, predictably began falling months before the onset of that long recession. For perspective, the stock index ranged above the 1060 level in January 1973 and was as low as about 780 in December of that year before it reached its final recessionary nadir of 577.60 near the end of 1974 (again predictably, several months before the beginning of a new up-phase in the business cycle).

The Granville advice, within this bleak business-cycle framework, provides intriguing reading. On December 27, 1972, with share prices near a cyclical peak and about to start skidding, the technical analyst advised subscribers that "clear sailing" lay ahead. In April of 1973, with the traditional prerecessionary slide in share prices under way, Mr. Granville advised that "stocks are on the bargain counter." In late June, he predicted that there was "an explosive rise ahead." On November 16, 1973, he wrote: "Technical evidence overwhelmingly bullish." By then, the Dow Jones average had fallen some 200 points from its January high level. As the recession deepened—a development that anyone watching any of the key leading indicators discussed earlier, in Chapter 9, would have foreseen—the stock average sank nearly another 300 points.

In early 1974, with the recession still continuing, the Granville optimism persisted. On January 25, 1974, the analyst proclaimed: "Now is the time to buy." On April 5 of that year, he asserted that "great days lie ahead" and that "December 5, 1973, marked the major Dow bottom." On that day, the average closed at 788.31, more than 200 points above its ultimate recessionary low point. In a final burst of misguided optimism, on June 14, 1974, Mr. Granville affirmed "the new bull market." The recession had nine more months to go at that time, in fact, and anyone following the important statistical indicators already outlined wouldn't yet have seen any light at the recessionary tunnel's end. Between June and December of 1974, the Dow Jones average fell from closing high of 859.67 to a closing low, as noted in Chapter 5, of 577.60.

Too much can possibly be read into this brief history of Mr. Granville in the 1973–75 recession. His record contains forecasting triumphs as well as the failures outlined above. But the point to be made is that this is not something for the do-it-yourself investor to be focusing on. Nor will any effort be made here to explain the sort of complicated analytic techniques that underlie the broad conclusions of Mr. Granville and dozens of other technical analysts. Your time is precious. Use what of it you can to keep abreast of the business cycle and the secular trends discussed earlier that can also affect stock prices in a major way.

For similar reasons, such relatively sophisticated market tactics as stock-option trading should probably be eschewed by the do-it-yourselfer. Suffice it to be aware that a stock option is a contract that gives the owner the right to buy or sell a specific number of shares, usually 100, of a particular stock at a fixed price within a prescribed period of time. For the privilege of the option, the buyer pays a "premium." An option conveying the right to buy stock with the option's seller, or "writer," is known as a "call" because it allows the buyer to call stock away from the writer. An option conveying the right to sell stock to the writer is termed a "put" because it allows the buyer to sell the stock to the writer. Either action by the buyer is referred to as "exercising" the option.

Option-trading techniques demand a close scrutiny of your option holdings and can become an extremely complicated and risky business. Again, the best approach is to steer clear of this time-consuming endeavor and instead devote your fullest attention to the fundamentals already discussed.

In December 1980 *Business Week* magazine published a long article titled "How to Play the Options Game." While the article explained in reasonably simple language the rudiments of option trading, it also warned that "most people who dabble in options" at an "elementary" level wind up losing money. It quotes a Philadelphia stockbroker who traded options as conceding that "there are three things that can happen to the options speculator, and two of them are bad. If the stock does what the speculator expects, he wins. But if it stays the same or moves against him, he loses."

Options are but one of a number of relatively sophisticated investment tactics associated with the stock market. Such tactics multiply in other investment areas, ranging from real-estate buying to something—recently deemed illegal—called "commodity tax straddles." As a general rule, you should steer clear, even where illegality is not an issue, unless you have a great amount of time to devote to investing and more than a tidbit of gambling instinct in you.

On a more practical level, when you've done your homework on the business cycle, you can better spend your hours considering how best to invest in the stock market without gambling on such devices as options. Again, advice is to keep it simple.

Picking a Broker

If you invest in the stock market, quite obviously you will require the services of a stockbroker, unless you intend to purchase for yourself a seat on the New York Stock Exchange. To do that, you would need a very large amount of money and time to devote to your stock-market activities. If you lack these, find yourself a stockbroker who is readily available by phone and won't be trying to run your portfolio for you—in short, a good order taker. You may wish to deal with one of Wall Street's giants, in the understandable conviction that there is safety in size. If so, such names as Merrill Lynch, Paine Webber, Shearson, and E. F. Hutton spring to mind. Or you may wish to save a bit of commission money and deal instead through a so-called discount broker—someone like Charles Schwab, Quick & Reilly, or Discount Brokerage. A 1979 study shows that the commission on a purchase of 100 shares of International Business Machines stock was $30 if the transaction was handled by Discount Brokerage and $88 if handled through Merrill Lynch.

In the final analysis, the key question becomes whether you feel comfortable with a particular broker. If you feel happier with the Merrill Lynch fellow who charges $88 than with the Discount Brokerage man who is $58 cheaper, you may want to forget about the extra cost and stay with the person you are most comfortable with. Whatever you decide, bear in mind that all you really need from any broker is efficient, faithful, reliable execution of orders and accountability. As a do-it-yourself investor, who probably knows a good deal more about the business cycle than 99 percent of the nation's stockbroker community, there's absolutely no reason for you to worry about additional brokerage services. Bare-bones execution is all you need. In brief, be your own decision maker, but remember that you will need a reliable, readily available broker to carry out those decisions. As for safety, you can easily rent a safe-deposit box and put your stock certificates in it; your dividend checks will be automatically mailed to you, usually quarterly, by the particular company. You'll also receive its annual reports and, more than likely, other company information from time to time. Some firms send stockholders company magazines at no extra cost. One such magazine, a very good one, is sent around by Du Pont. It contains articles of wide-ranging interest, not just pro-Du Pont propaganda.

13.
Fixed-income Investing

So far, our attention has focused mainly on common-stock, or equity, investments. There is, of course, a huge other type of securities investment that the do-it-yourselfer shouldn't overlook in mapping a strategy geared to the business cycle. It's called the "fixed-income market." It's actually far larger than the equity market, but tends to receive less attention because it's usually duller, lacking the volatility and excitement of the stock market.

A share of stock may split or its dividend may change with a change in earnings prospects. As a stockholder, you own a piece of the action. You are a proprietor, however small your investment may be in the enterprise in question, however vast its sales and earnings may be. Not so when you decide to invest money in a fixed-income security. Then you become a lender, not a part owner of anything, and in return for that loan you receive a fixed income, or rate of interest, that is paid at regular, prescribed intervals. The enterprise in question may experience extreme good fortune, and perhaps the per-share dividend it pays its shareholders each quarter will double and redouble. But that interest rate normally stays the same. You're stuck with it—which naturally won't be such a bad thing if the company's sales begin to slide instead of rise and its earnings and dividend payments go sharply down instead of up.

Most investors tend to keep at least some fixed-income securities within their nest eggs, along with common stocks. The precise percentage should vary according to a variety of factors. These range from an individual's particular circumstances—age, long-range plans, other earnings, and so on—to such secular considerations as the degree and likely persistence of inflation. We won't try to tell you just what breakdown is best suited for you. The important point to understand here, and it cannot be overemphasized, is this: that it's possible to gear your fixed-income investing to the ups and downs of the business cycle just as profitably as we have seen is possible with stock-market investments.

In the discussion of the stock market's relationship to the business cycle, it was stressed that different types of stocks tend to respond in different ways to the cyclical ups and downs of the economy. The same thing is true with fixed-income securities. The difference, however, is that here the crucial consideration involves such matters as the length of the debt issue— that is, when it matures—and whether the issuer happens to be a corporation, as in the stock-market situation, or some other entity, such as a unit of government.

In trying to decide how best to invest in a fixed-income security, then, your primary concern once again must be: How will the business cycle affect this investment? And to answer that, you must once again pay attention to the relationship of interest rates to the economy's ups and downs. When interest rates rise, prices of fixed-income securities decline, and vice versa. This may sound complicated, but it's really obvious. Suppose that you buy a corporate bond valued at $1,000 and paying yearly interest of $100. The bond's interest rate would be 10 percent. But now suppose that its price falls from the original $1,000 level to $500. Its yearly interest, normally paid in the form of cashable coupons that can be clipped every six months from the bond, is still $100. But the interest rate—$100 as a percent of $500—would now amount to 20 percent. Or let's suppose instead that the bond's price jumps to $2,000. The interest rate then—$100 as a percent of $2,000—would be only 5 percent. To repeat: When interest rates rise, prices of fixed-income securities decline, and vice versa.

As a general rule, as we've noted, interest rates behave as a lagging economic indicator. They tend to keep rising in the early months of a recession and tend to keep falling in the early months of an economic recovery. In this way, they generally behave in much the same manner as outlays for new plants and equipment.

With this knowledge as a starting point, it's possible to construct a prudent investment strategy for fixed-income investing. The time to buy such a security, clearly, is when interest rates are near a cyclical peak and fixed-income security prices are close to a bottom point. Using business-cycle common sense, we see that this would be some time after a recession has begun, but well before any up-phase of the business cycle appears on the horizon. And the time to sell, just as obviously, is when interest rates are around their cyclical lows and the security prices are around their highs. Again, with business-cycle logic, we can readily deduce that selling is best done not precisely when a recession is about to end, but a while later, when the economy in general is well along on a new recovery road.

Within this general framework, a few footnotes should be inserted. Fixed-income securities vary among other ways by length of maturity. Longer-term securities—what we call "bonds"—can stretch in maturity all the way up to many decades before the loan in question must be repaid in full. Others, generally called "notes," can extend up to several years in maturity. Still others, such as Treasury bills, usually range under a year.

Rates and Cycles

Now, let's take a closer look at the relationship between interest rates and the business cycle, and see how the prudent do-it-

FIXED-INCOME INVESTING

yourself investor in fixed-income securities can put an understanding of this link to the fullest use. Let's first consider the relationship between short-term interest rates and the business cycle. Specifically, let's look at the behavior of rates on Treasury bills carrying a three-month maturity. Usually, we see by the record, these rates have kept right on climbing after the onset of a recession—not always, but nearly always. Only twice in the post-World War II era—in 1953 and again in 1960—did rates on three-month Treasury bills begin to edge down before a recession set in. More typical, for instance, were the patterns evident in 1973 and 1980. Then, these short-term rates kept rising for eight months after the onset of the 1973–75 recession and for five months after the start of the 1980 recession. On the average, over the postwar period, rates on three-month Treasury bills have kept climbing for approximately two months into recessions before sliding along with economic activity in general.

The behavior of long-term interest rates is similar. These rates, represented typically by top-rated corporate bonds, have also kept rising, on the average, for some two months after the onset of recessions during the postwar era.

Once rates begin to slide in a recession, the decline tends to be considerable. A study by Argus Research Corp., a New York-based investment service, finds that short-term rates fell nearly 50 percent on the average during four recent postwar slumps. The comparable recessionary drop for long-term rates, the study shows, works out to about 15 percent. Long-term rates tend generally to be less volatile than short-term rates; their more modest declines have usually followed more moderate increases as recessions have developed.

A distinctive pattern is also evident after a recession ends and the economy embarks once again along a recovery road. The 1969–70 recession ended in November 1970, but the Treasury-bill interest rate did not hit bottom until early 1972, after more than a year of business expansion. Similarly, when the 1973–75 recession ended in March 1975, the bill rate did not hit bottom until the start of 1977, nearly two years after the slump had ended and a new up-phase of the business cycle had begun.

Earlier in the postwar era, these time lags were often shorter, but they generally existed, and investors who understood them were in a good position to profit through that knowledge.

A similar timing pattern is apparent for long-term rates. For instance, after the 1973–75 recession, rates on top-rated corporate bonds hit bottom almost precisely when Treasury-bill rates were also at a postrecessionary low point. Exceptions to this timing, the record shows, have been municipal-bond rates. These, on the average, did not hit bottom after the 1973–75 recession until the start of 1978, a full year after corporate bond rates were at a nadir.

It's clear that a high degree of business-cycle predictability persists throughout the fixed-income market. And it's clear that, for all the troubles that have plagued the fixed-income market in recent years of high inflation, money could have been made there with proper attention to business-cycle timing. If you doubt this, glance at Figures 13 and 14, charts adapted from *BCD*, which trace various interest rates over a quarter-century span. Note how in every instance rate movements were strongly affected by turns in the business cycle (as usual, the recessions are indicated by shading).

Underlying a strategy of tying fixed-income investing to the business cycle is the aim of nailing down profits on price changes. And these can be considerable. Let's suppose once again that a corporate bond is issued at $1,000 with a coupon that pays a yearly interest amounting to $100, or 10 percent of the bond's initial value. Now, let's suppose that interest rates generally rise. The yield on the bond's coupon rises to, say, 15 percent from the original 10 percent. To yield 15 percent, the bond would have to sell at only about $666, or $334 less than its original price. Suppose further that you have decided, on the basis of some do-it-yourself watching of the business cycle, that the economy is in the early stages of a recession—so early, in fact, that bond rates haven't yet peaked and gone into their traditional late- and postrecessionary slide. Against this business-cycle background, you decide to buy the bond in question at

FIXED-INCOME INVESTING 145

FIGURE 13

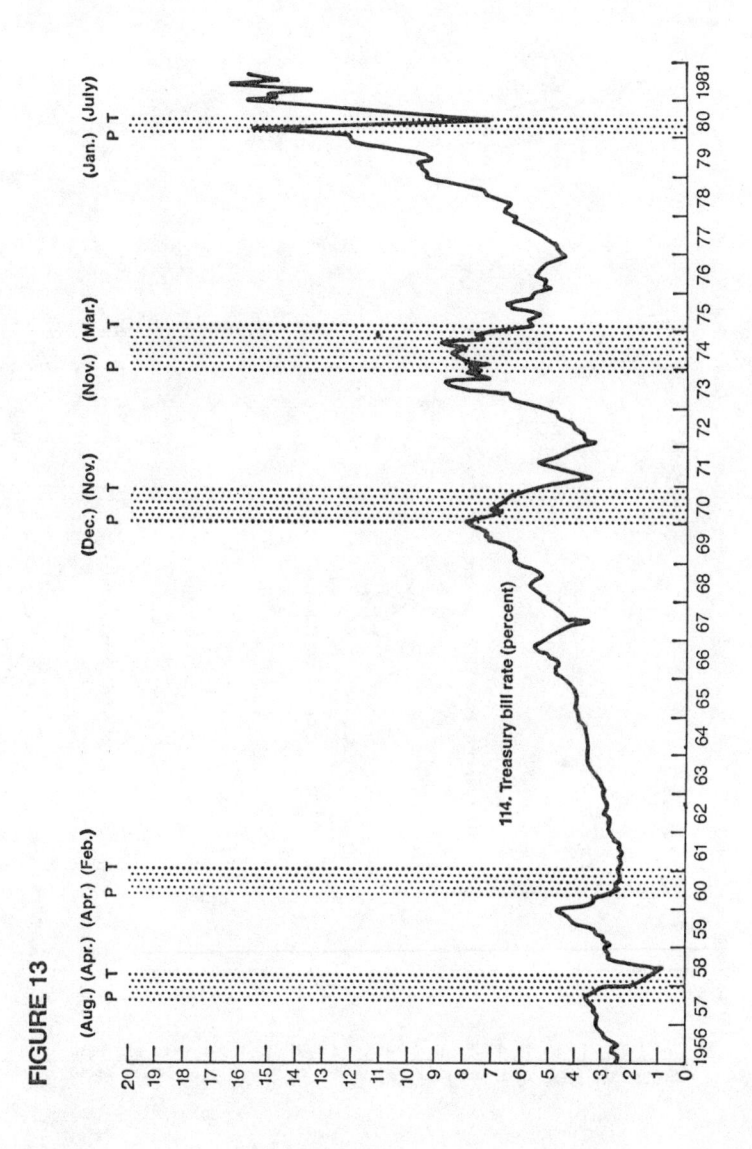

114. Treasury bill rate (percent)

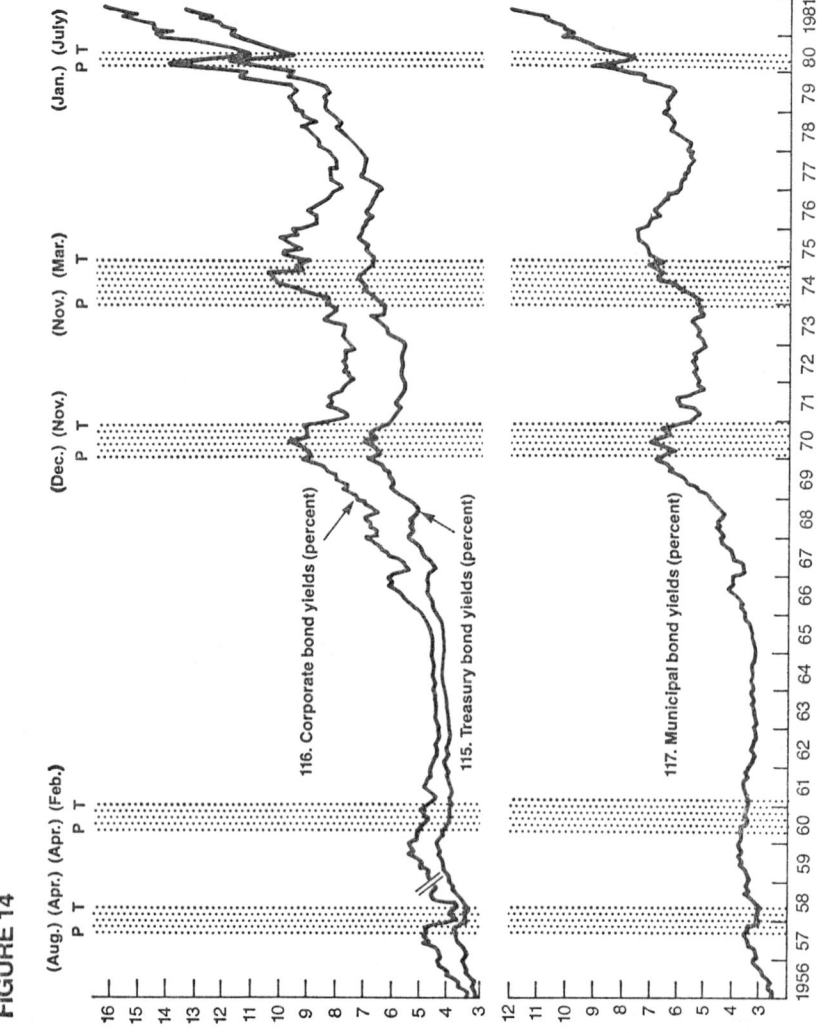

FIGURE 14

$666. You aren't buying it so much to take advantage of the 15 percent yield on its coupon as, basically, to capitalize on the anticipated price improvement once interest rates begin to decline as the recession nears an end. By definition, as rates on fixed-income securities go down, prices go up—and, of course, vice versa. Business-cycle experience suggests that it is unlikely, returning to our $666 bond, that you would see a five-percentage-point drop in the yield, all the way back down to 10 percent. But the record makes clear that a large fraction of such a decline, over the course of a business-cycle turnaround, is entirely likely even in the face of a long-term worsening inflation. For instance, within a three-month period in 1980—by no coincidence, the latter months of the 1980 recession—the average yield on new issues of highly rated corporate bonds fell from about 14 percent to about 11 percent. Going back to our $666 bond purchase, a drop to 11 percent in rates would translate into a market price for the bond of above $910. That's a gain on your investment of $244, or about 36 percent in a period of roughly three months.

It's apparent in the above illustration that investing for yield, per se, isn't the objective. Sharply changing interest rates are simply a manifestation of sharp price changes. It's also apparent that this bond investment isn't something that can be put away in your safe-deposit box and forgotten about—not when its value can change nearly 40 percent in about three months. A final point: The space of time covered in our illustration hardly qualifies as typical. The year 1980 was a time of high inflation, a sharp but short recession, a brief imposition of credit controls by the Carter administration and, as a result of all this, exceptionally volatile interest-rate changes. We noted earlier, for instance, that short-term bill rates tend to behave with even more volatility than long-term bond rates, and this was readily apparent in the 1980 recession. In the period when the interest rate on our sample bond fell three percentage points, the average rate on three-month Treasury bills plunged nearly nine percentage points—from nearly 16 percent to less than 7 percent; other short-term interest rates behaved in a similar fashion. Quite obviously, the potential profits are even greater when one is dealing with fixed-income securities of short maturity.

And so, of course, is the risk of losses. If you should happen to mistime your investment moves by only a month or two, you could end up with a loss, rather than a fat gain. As Figures 13 and 14 show, turns in interest-rate trends can be extra-steep when they come. Also, particularly with regard to the shorter-term securities, aberrations can occur, especially when inflation is running high. An investor who plunged into Treasury bills early in 1980 would only have managed a large gain on the investment if he had pulled out of the investment extra early in a subsequent up-phase of the business cycle. We have observed that interest rates generally keep falling for many months after a recession has begun. But, with the supershort recession of 1980, the inevitable upturn in rates occurred much sooner than usual. By early 1981 the average rate of Treasury bills was back up above the 15 percent mark, yet the recession had been over only about half a year.

The Inflation Factor

Up to now, we've limited our discussion of fixed-income investing to business-cycle considerations. But there obviously is another major factor to be weighed—whether to invest in fixed-income securities at all or to stick, for example, to the equity market. We've stressed that the do-it-yourself investor must try to avoid getting into a portfolio situation where constant monitoring of each investment becomes necessary. It should be apparent, from the examples cited above, that the fixed-income market can be an exceedingly tricky investment area when inflation is severe. For this reason, you would probably be best advised to hold such purchases to a minimum. There are, of course, ways to avail oneself of high interest rates at times when inflation is excessive. But buying a particular corporate bond issue doesn't seem to be the safest way to do that. Rather, it's possible to invest in highly liquid mutual-fund shares that concentrate their holdings in an assortment of short-term securities, including notably Treasury bills. Of course, if rates drop sharply and suddenly, so ultimately will the return that you receive from the money-market mutual fund, as these entities are called.

A sensible procedure, perhaps, is to examine the long-term price outlook, without regard for business-cycle considerations. If you decide that inflation is severe and likely to stay bad over the long term, then investing in fixed-income securities would appear a relatively high-risk proposition. If you want to tap the high yields available, you probably should stick to the liquidity available through a large money-market fund. Many of these funds are listed regularly in *The Wall Street Journal* and other major newspapers. They are offered through major banks and brokerage houses. They advertise frequently, giving phone numbers to call for detailed information on how to open such accounts. Merrill Lynch and Dreyfus are among the larger, well-established securities firms offering a variety of such funds. By investing in these money-market funds, you will be keeping your money in extremely short-term securities and receiving, when interest rates on such securities are high, a handsome rate of return on what amounts to a cash holding.

On the other hand, if severe inflation doesn't appear to be an overriding consideration in the long-term outlook, there are some sensible ways to weigh a fixed-income investment against a purchase of stock.

Let's take a closer look: Should one put money into the stock market or into, say, a fixed-income security with a relatively long maturity, such as a corporate bond?

Let's assume that the do-it-yourself investor, the person asking the question, has dutifully studied the business-cycle climate. He or she has perused the key leading indicators and is well aware of such vital considerations as the usual behavior of share prices and interest rates at particular phases of the business cycle.

Should this investor put that extra $10,000 legacy from Aunt Millie into the stock market? Or into the bond market? He or she wants to do one or the other, but isn't quite sure which. And from a business-cycle point of view, either alternative seems to offer promise.

Earlier in this chapter, we indicated that fixed-income investments are likely to entail a greater amount of watching than equity investments. So, on that basis alone, let's score a point for the stock market. But what else should we be thinking about?

One thing, quite obviously, is the return to investors. We've previously discussed dividends and interest and how they are alike and how they differ. Now, let's take a closer glance at the comparison of the two. Let's compare, for example, the average dividend-yield to stockholders over the year of the 500 stocks contained in the Standard & Poor's common-stock index, and the average interest paid by top-rated corporate bonds (we'll have more to say about bond ratings later).

In theory, bond owning is a safer proposition than stock owning. A bondholder, theoretically, is guaranteed a fixed rate of return on his investment. A stockholder's fortunes, in contrast, tend to ride with the fortunes of the company involved; if its earnings soar, so most likely will the stockholder's dividends, and vice versa.

Since bond holding, in theory, carries an extra degree of safety, one would suppose that the interest return on, say, $10,000 invested in a corporate bond would tend to be lower—the safety factor—than the equivalent dividend yield on $10,000 of stock investment in the same company. And once upon a time—before the 1960s—that was indeed the situation. But not in later years—and for good reason. Bond interest levels since the 1960s have almost invariably exceeded comparable dividend yields, often by as much as 100 percent, notwithstanding the supposedly high riskiness, on a relative basis, of stock investing. The reason, quite simply, is that with inflation, bond owning becomes a riskier investment game than buying equities. Remember that the interest rate on a bond, especially one that won't mature for thirty years or so, won't normally be rising along with inflation. But a company's earnings—and therefore its dividend payout—will be increasing, however cheapened may be the value of the paid-out dollars. Thus we see that inflation turns an important segment of the investment world upside down. A relatively risky investment becomes less risky—and therefore pays out less of a return to investors than an investment that, in an inflation-free world, would be relatively riskless.

Ultimately, the choice between investing in the stock market and investing in corporate bonds or some other fixed-income vehicle entails a good deal more than simply comparing the respective rates of return. In an inflationary era, the bond may yield more per dollar invested than the stock. But remember that the yield is fixed and won't rise, as a dividend payment well might, if the inflation rate ratchets upward.

The inflation rate may not ratchet upward. Indeed, inflation may not be a problem at the time any such investment decision is being made. In that case, a gap between interest and dividend yields should obviously be given considerable weight in any decision as to whether to place money into bonds or stocks. But if inflation is a problem, and possibly a growing one, the matter of relatively high interest versus relatively low dividend yield hardly can be construed as the overriding consideration.

A Word About Ratings

There are three major security-rating agencies—Moody's Investors Service, Standard & Poor's Corp., and Fitch Investors Service. These three agencies have published securities ratings in one form or another for over fifty years. Ratings, indeed, have become part of the language of Wall Street. There is no magic formula for determining ratings. The various rating agencies stress that each case is different. The final decision on how to rate a fixed-income security results from an analysis of many factors and tends to be judgmental. However, there are certain key considerations. Among them:

What are the management's objectives and how do they plan to achieve them? What are the management's financial and operating policies? Has management provided for unforeseen events? Do the particular companies demonstrate an ability to earn good returns consistently? Do the companies' balance sheets—their liquidity positions—look healthy?

Here is a brief description of how one of these agencies—Standard & Poor's—defines bond ratings. Bonds rated AAA are highest-grade obligations. They possess the ultimate degree of protection as to principle and interest. In market terms, they tend to move with the general trend of interest rates. Bonds rated AA are also deemed quality obligations and in the majority of instances differ from AAA issues only in small degree. Bonds rated A are regarded as upper-medium grade. They have considerable investment strength but aren't entirely free from adverse effects of changes in economic and trade conditions. Interest and principle are regarded as safe. They predominantly reflect money rates in their market behavior, but to some extent, they also mirror economic conditions. The BBB, or medium-grade, category is borderline between clearly sound obligations and ones where the speculative element begins to predominate. This group, traditionally, has been the lowest qualifying for commercial-bank investment portfolios. Bonds given a BB rating are regarded as lower medium grade. They have only minor investment characteristics and tend to be more speculative. Bonds rated B are deemed speculative and payment of interest cannot be assured under difficult economic conditions. Bonds rated CCC and CC are outright speculations, with the lower rating denoting the more speculative. Interest is paid, but continuation is questionable in periods of poor economic conditions. The rating of C is reserved for income bonds on which no interest is being paid. All bonds rated DDD, DD, and D are in default, with the rating indicating the relative salvage value. The least salvagable of these are those with the D rating.

The other two rating services have similar arrangements. Above and beyond the discussion in this chapter regarding purchase of fixed-income securities, one must also be wary of a bond's safety, as seen through its particular rating, whether by

Moody's, Standard & Poor's, or Fitch. The result of the rating system, as a general rule, is that the bonds or other fixed-income securities with the highest ratings tend, dollar for dollar, to carry a lower interest rate than those with lower ratings, which are also more speculative.

The Tax Angle

A word should also be inserted with regard to tax considerations. Generally, dividends paid on common stock of a financially healthy company are fully taxable. That's also normally true on the interest paid on a bond of a financially healthy corporation. However, the prudent investor should also be aware that the tax status of a particular investment tends to vary more widely within the fixed-income market. While corporate-bond interest, like dividend yield, is normally fully taxable, interest on municipal securities—those issued by state or local government units—is normally exempt from federal taxation. It may also be exempt from local taxation if the investor happens to reside within the state of issue. Thus, a New York State resident who buys a New York City fixed-income security would not have to pay federal, state, or city tax on the interest gained. A Minnesota resident holding the same security would be exempt only from federal taxation on the interest.

The other broad category of fixed-income securities that offers a tax break, albeit a lesser one, is that where the issuer is the U.S. Treasury. When you own a short-term Treasury bill, a medium-term Treasury note, or a long-term Treasury bond, the interest received is normally exempt from state and local— but not from federal—taxation. This can become a significant consideration if one resides, say, in New York City, where state and local taxation levels are relatively high. For example: One investor may earn interest on a corporate bond of $100 a year, while another investor owns a Treasury bond paying a like amount. Both live in New York. Both are in the same tax bracket. But the investor getting $100 from the corporate bond under law must pay a fraction of that investment income to the New York State Income Tax Bureau. The other investor doesn't because states and cities can't tax income from Treasury securities.

Whatever the fixed-income security under investment consideration, its interest rate will tend to reflect, along with many other things, the tax factor. For instance, the interest rate on a tax-free security will naturally tend to be lower, all other things being equal, than the interest rate on an otherwise comparable, but fully taxable, corporate security. Like the matter of ratings, the tax factor constitutes one more consideration to be weighed before any decision is made to enter the fixed-income market. To repeat, one's primary concern must be the business cycle and its relationship to interest rate trends. However, particularly when one ponders the fixed-income market, other tangential factors cannot be neglected.

Unfixed Issues

Up to now, this chapter's discussion has focused on fixed-income securities. In times of high inflation, such as the early 1980s, securities carrying fixed-interest rates are at a distinct disadvantage. A 7 percent interest rate may seem dandy, if prices are rising 2 percent a year. But not if the price rise accelerates to 15 percent a year. You're still stuck with the 7 percent interest rate, which in "real" terms, of course, becomes a rate of *minus* 8 percent. Not surprisingly, to attract investors during severe inflations, some fixed-income securities become, in effect, unfixed. That is, the interest rate may be allowed by the issuer to vary. Another tactic of the issuer is to offer to redeem the bond at maturity for some form of tangible asset rather than simply for cash. In 1980, for example, Sunshine Mining Co., a silver producer, sold two issues of bonds that are redeemable either for $1,000 of cash or for fifty ounces of silver or its cash equivalent, whichever proves to be greater in 1995, the maturity date. The bonds—which were announced in such papers as *The Wall Street Journal*—carry an interest rate of 8.5 percent, which by no coincidence happened to be relatively modest compared with interest levels prevailing in 1980 on comparable, conventional corporate bonds. Such arrangements remain the exception, but it's well to be aware that not all bond-type securities are sold strictly on the basis of a fixed-interest rate, paid in cash.

How to Buy

As a general rule, you can go about buying a fixed-income security in much the same way that you would buy a share of stock—through a stockbroker. You'll be charged a commission, of course, that will vary according to which broker you work through. As noted, some brokers—for example, the discount houses that offer few other services to customers—normally charge less to execute a given transaction than other brokerage firms.

One distinction between buying shares of stock and certain fixed-income securities, however, is that you don't always have to go through a broker to purchase the latter. You can, literally, do it yourself if you want, for instance, to buy a Treasury bill. You can submit a so-called tender, or letter, to your particular branch of the Federal Reserve System. In New York City, that would be the New York Federal Reserve Bank at 33 Liberty Street, New York, New York 10045. Your tender, or letter, to the Fed must specify the amount of bills that you want to buy, as well as such other information as the maturity date you desire and whether you will want to reinvest, or "roll over," the funds when the bills become due. Full details about how to go about such a do-it-yourself investment can be obtained by writing to your local Federal Reserve Bank. A similar do-it-yourself procedure is possible if you want to buy Treasury notes or Treasury bonds.

While through most of this book I have encouraged you to do things yourself, I must confess at this point that I'm dubious about trying to buy fixed-income securities on a do-it-yourself basis, even if you are dealing with an organization as prestigious as the Federal Reserve System. You will save a few dollars in brokerage commissions, but it's a time-consuming business and can occasionally pose unforeseen problems. For instance, in 1979 thousands of owners of Treasury bills that had matured complained that checks due them on the investments were two to three weeks late in coming from the government. A Treasury official blamed the costly delays on a computer foul-up in Washington and delays in the Washington mailing system. In general, Treasury securities bought through a broker or bank would be left in the custody of the particular institution and any such headaches would fall on that institution's shoulders. It's worth the commission cost. In this one instance, therefore, the advice is don't do it yourself.

14.
Tangibles

UP TO THIS POINT, OUR ATTENTION HAS FOCUSED MAINLY ON INvesting in securities, be they stocks or bonds or Treasury bills or whatever else. We've been talking, essentially, about buying or selling pieces of paper, security certificates that signify, with their finely etched artwork, the ownership of a tiny fraction of a corporation or an indebtedness on the part of some public or private borrower. And we have seen how a familiarity with the ups and downs of the business cycle can provide the key to timing the purchase or sale of such security investments.

In a society such as modern America's, where the rule of law, however imperfectly, prevails, security-type investments over the long haul seem the most sensible kind for the prudent layman who hasn't the time or inclination to become an expert on Oriental rugs or stamps or toy soldiers or, for that matter, gold coins. But that is not to say that one should wholly disregard the importance of what are called "tangibles" as an investment possibility. What do we mean here by "tangibles"? Quite simply, things that can be touched, held in the hand, or carried on a truck or railroad car. Gold coins are tangibles. So are silver and copper and diamonds. And, moving away from the mineral kingdom, so are soybeans and cattle and hogs and sugar and land. And so is a Rembrandt painting or a Chippendale chair.

Investing in tangibles can't be ignored particularly in times of worsening inflation, when prices keep climbing regardless of business-cycle developments. As the value of a currency diminishes during a prolonged price spiral, the price of most tangible assets naturally tends to increase. If you are fortunate in your investment choice, your particular asset will rise in price even more sharply than prices generally, and from an investment point of view, you will be well ahead of the game. However, as we will see, picking the right asset can be an exceedingly tricky business, even if you are familiar with the particular item, be it gold, silver, stamps, or whatever.

Before taking a closer look at the investment peculiarities of various tangibles, however, let's first conduct a broader inspection of how tangibles generally behave within a business-cycle framework. A starting place is a relatively obscure BCD economic indicator. It goes by the cumbersome title of "Spot-market Prices, Raw Materials." It measures the spot-market price movements of various raw materials on commodity markets and organized exchanges. The commodities include burlap, copper scrap, cotton, hides, lead scrap, print cloth, rosin, rubber, steel scrap, tallow, tin, wool tops, and zinc. Such items are purposely selected for the index because they are widely used for further processing, freely traded in the open market, particularly sensitive to changing supply-demand conditions in those markets, and sufficiently standardized so that their prices have been regularly quoted over many years.

Thus we see that this particular price index presents a reasonably typical reflection of commodity-price movements in general. Moreover, because its history can be traced in *Business Conditions Digest*, we can further determine precisely how its ups and downs relate to those of the economy as a whole. The relationship is marked. The index generally behaves as a leading indicator, tending to move up or down ahead of general business activity. Reasonably typical is its behavior during the recession of 1960–61. While the recession didn't set in until April of 1960, the index had peaked in January. And it hit bottom in the fall of 1960, even though business as a whole didn't begin to turn around until February 1961.

Like many economic barometers, this price index hasn't always foreshadowed business cycle trends reliably. It kept climbing, for example, in the early months of the 1973–75 recession. The index generally has proved more reliable in signaling business upturns than recessions.

Nonetheless, the index's general performance over many decades offers a valuable guideline for anyone seeking to invest in a wide array of tangibles, particularly those commodities that go into the general production process. The indicator teaches that the time to sell is several months before a recession sets in and that the time to buy is before an economic recovery develops. Indeed, it can be said that a prudent commodities strategy fits into the same broad sort of business-cycle framework as, say, a prudent stock-market strategy. As in buying stocks, the precise timing will depend to a degree on what particular item is being considered for purchase or sale. But the general rule remains: Sell before a business-cycle peak occurs and buy while a recession remains in progress.

A Prudent Course

We noted earlier that investing in tangibles can't be ignored in eras of worsening inflation that transcend the ups and downs of the business cycle. While the importance of business-cycle timing should never be wholly neglected, it becomes a good deal less crucial if one can safely conclude that there exists a long-term trend toward higher and higher rates of inflation. If you can make that judgment—by applying the proper analysis, outlined in Chapter 7, to detect such a secular development—then the prudent course may well be to forget about the business cycle and simply stick with whatever tangibles you decide to purchase.

The wisdom of such a course in a time of worsening inflation was clearly demonstrated in a 1980 study by Salomon Brothers, the large New York-based securities concern. It calculated the average annual rate of return on fourteen different types of investments over the preceding decade, a time of generally severe inflation. The study found that gold and oil brought the highest returns in the ten years, each showing rates of 31.6 percent annually. The remaining investments, in order of their annual percentage rates of return, were silver (23.7), U.S. stamps (21.8), Chinese ceramics (18.8), rare books (16.1), U.S. coins (16), diamonds (15.1), old masters (13.4), U.S. farmland (12.6), housing (10.2), foreign exchange (7.55), stocks (6.8), and bonds (6.4). For perspective, the consumer price index rose at an annual rate of 7.7 percent during that decade.

The study, tongue in cheek, adds:

> The fascination with tangibles reached a zenith recently when a news service featured a story stating that the mineral content of the human body is now worth $7.28, compared to 98¢ at the beginning of the last decade, thereby providing a 10-year compounded average annual rate of return of 22%. The prudent investor will note, of course, that federal law presently prohibits purchase or sale or liquidation in any form of the mineral-bearing vehicle.

As the study suggests, while tangibles generally fare well during prolonged price spirals, the pattern is by no means uniform. Let's now take a closer look at the peculiarities of specific tangibles.

Gold

Gold, which, with oil, tops the Salomon Brothers list, is a logical place to begin.

Investing in gold, we have seen in my dealings with Perry Flynn (see Chapter 6), can be accomplished in the familiar manner of buying stocks in companies that mine the metal. Most of these concerns, not surprisingly, are situated in South Africa. But others are also available for stockownership—for instance, Homestake Mining Company in the United States, headquartered in San Francisco, and various similar outfits based in Canada whose shares may be purchased, like Homestake, on the New York Stock Exchange or on the American Stock Exchange through a simple phone call to your friendly neighborhood stockbroker—plus, of course, a commission fee. That is not the sort of gold investing, however, to be discussed in this review of tangible investment vehicles. There is the obvious distinction between owning a piece of paper that states your fractional interest in a gold mine some four thousand or five thousand miles away, or perhaps farther, and owning a gold coin or ingot that resides in your wall safe or your safe-deposit box at the bank around the corner.

And there are subtler, far trickier distinctions. For example, let's imagine that Mr. Smith has a $10,000 investment in the stock of a South African gold-mining concern and Mr. Jones has $10,000 invested in gold coins kept in his local safe-deposit box. For years, the value of the two investments has tended to move similarly, up together by about the same amount and, rarely while inflation has raged, down together by about the same amount. But now let's suppose that a race war erupts in South Africa and that the subsequent turmoil is such that the operations at the gold mine in which Mr. Smith owns stock grind to a near halt for a long period. The mine's earnings obviously will sink or vanish. Indeed, a sizable loss develops for the year, and much of the company's facilities are damaged in the fighting. It's no surprise that the market price of the company's shares plummets. Mr. Smith is in trouble with his investment.

But what's happened to Mr. Jones' investment? Because of the turmoil in South Africa, by far the largest gold-producing area in the world, output of the yellow metal generally drops sharply. As the supply of new gold shrivels while demand for it holds steady, the metal's price begins to move up sharply. Responding to basic supply-demand forces, it doubles, so that the value of Mr. Jones' investment climbs to $20,000. Meanwhile, consider poor Mr. Smith's situation, with a piece of paper—his certificate of ownership in the ill-fated mine—worth, say $5,000, or half its prior value.

The chance of political strife in South Africa, it should be added, is by no means the sole possibility tending to distinguish investing in gold the metal from investing in a gold-mining company as a stockholder. Other potential developments that could adversely affect stockowners range from the distant threat of nationalization of such enterprises to natural disasters such as flooding of mines, to poor management at a particular company.

None of these concerns may be worrying Mr. Jones. However, he will have some worries of his own. His wall safe, if that's where he keeps his gold, could be burglarized. Or, if he keeps his gold at the local bank, his safe-deposit box could be sealed as a result of some banking panic that might prompt such drastic governmental action. Most important, the gold, wherever it is stored, won't be paying Mr. Jones any interest; the metal of course pays no interest. Mr. Smith, in contrast, was collecting some fat dividend checks from his gold mine before the trouble erupted.

The prudent do-it-yourself investor, in brief, should clearly understand the pros and cons of holding gold as a tangible as opposed to investing in the metal through the stock-market route. Once these are understood, what are the avenues available along the tangible route and how, within a business-cycle framework, should they be approached?

Gold can be purchased, of course, in the form of bullion, which can provide a suitable form of gold holding for individuals of extensive means. Since bars may exceed four hundred troy ounces and gold in recent years has brought many hundreds of dollars a troy ounce in the marketplace, buying a single, standard-size bar would involve a scale of investment much grander than those on which this book focuses. However, smaller-size bars have recently become available for purchase by investors who are far from rich. A word of caution, however, should be sounded. Any gold bar, whatever its size, should be carefully checked and assayed by experts before purchase.

A more practical form of gold holding for the do-it-yourself investor is to buy gold coins. These naturally come in a wide variety. Some are rare and old, such as the many coins issued by the U.S. Government before President Franklin D. Roosevelt outlawed gold coinage in the early 1930s. Such coins carry what is commonly called a "numismatic premium" on top of the marketplace value of their gold content.

Another investment tactic would be to buy what are known as "bullion coins," such as the Austrian hundred-corona piece, the South African krugerrand, and the Mexican fifty-peso piece, none of which has an appreciable numismatic value. These are newer and relatively common, and this explains why they are relatively inexpensive, costing little more than the value of the gold of which they are made. Accordingly, if your interest in gold is strictly investment-oriented, without regard to such matters as coin rarity, the bullion-coin route makes the most sense. As in collecting any tangibles of rare quality, a special knowledge places one at a huge advantage, whether one is buying or selling. Unless you are prepared to become an expert on rare coins, you are best advised to eschew coin buying for reasons other than their gold content, and even that course carries risk. If you do decide to buy a coin that demands even a modest numismatic premium, you should have it authenticated by a reputable dealer. Or you can have it authenticated by the American Numismatic Association's Certification Service; if you want to do that, by agreement with the seller send the coin in question by registered mail to the ANA at 818 North Cascade Avenue, Colorado Springs, Colorado 80901, along with your estimate of the coin's value. In all, there are also more than forty newsletters and magazines that provide rare-coin investment lists, prices, and other information of interest to the specialist.

Once you get into the numismatic area, it's probable that a great deal of your time and energy will be used simply trying to keep tabs on the value of particular gold coins. And this, unfortunately, leaves less time for attention to business-cycle considerations. Again, that's the danger in going beyond investing in the yellow metal for its own sake and buying it instead in the sense of acquiring a "collectible" item, much as one might acquire a rare piece of furniture or an old master's painting.

If you must dabble in gold, try to focus on the metal's price performance, within the familiar framework of the business cycle. Leave numismatic matters to the coin experts.

The price of gold is not among the economic indicators that forecasters peruse continually for a sign of where the economy is heading, or is now, or has been. But that is not to say that no relationship exists between the price of gold and the ups and downs of the business cycle. One definitely does exist, the record shows, and it turns out to be a lagging relationship. The price of gold behaves much in the manner of a lagging economic indicator. In 1974, for instance, the price of gold on the London market rose from under $110 an ounce to nearly $200 an ounce. All the while, the economy was sliding further and further into a deep recession that was eventually to hit bottom in March of 1975. Once the London gold price began to slide around the start of 1975, the decline persisted far beyond the end of the 1973–75 recession. The gold-price nadir did not occur until the latter half of 1976, more than a year into the subsequent up-phase of the business cycle. When a price bottom finally was reached, it is noteworthy that the level almost precisely matched that recorded in late 1973, just as the 1973–75 recession was getting under way. The message needs no elaboration: Within a business-cycle framework, gold behaves as a lagging indicator and therefore should be sold only after a recession is clearly under way and bought only after an up-phase of the cycle is unmistakably in progress.

Before we move on to consider other tangibles, a thought should be inserted about investing in gold. We've covered buying the metal outright, as well as investing through stockownership in a gold-mining concern. There is also the gold-futures market, but that involves a degree of investment sophistication that, once again, goes beyond the focus of a book for the prudent do-it-yourselfer. However, very briefly, in the futures market, for example, Mr. Smith on January 13, may buy, say, ten

March futures contracts for a cash down payment of $30,000. Each contract controls 100 ounces of gold at, say, $573.50 an ounce. At the time of purchase, gold is selling at a cash price of $562 an ounce. By March 2 gold has climbed to $610 an ounce. Mr. Smith's ten contracts, now worth $610 an ounce, are sold for $610,000. This profit works out to $36,500—$610,000 minus $573,500—or a 122 percent return on the cash investment of $30,000. Of course, if the price of gold during the period in question were to plummet instead of rise, Mr. Smith would face losses, instead of a 122 percent gain. To repeat, this is an investment area best left to the sophisticated professional who is willing to spend a large quantity of time studying the intricacies of the gold futures market.

Some Alternatives

Of course, there are other tangibles that the do-it-yourself investor might prudently consider. We noted that oil, along with gold, topped the Salomon Brothers list, with a ten-year return amounting to 31.6 percent annually. Obviously oil, the commodity itself, isn't something that the average investor—who may have gold coins in storage—can buy and salt away in a safe-deposit box. The obvious, practical way for the layman to invest in oil is through the stock market, with the purchase of stock in one or another of the many publicly owned petroleum producers. Accordingly, for purposes of this discussion of tangible investments, oil can't seriously be included, other than to note the commodity's rather extraordinary relationship to the price of gold over the years. It's apparent, reviewing the long-term record, that an ounce of gold often has been worth somewhat less than twenty barrels of oil. This being the case, it's fair to say that oil prices and gold prices—whose business-cycle behavior we've already reviewed—move in rough tandem. In other words, oil prices, like gold prices, are apt to lag behind the ups and downs of the economy. Be warned, however, that given its extreme sensitivity to unpredictable developments on the political front, oil is hardly a commodity whose ups and downs can be anticipated simply through business-cycle analysis.

The same can be said, unfortunately, of a number of tangibles that are more readily available to the average investor. However, many other items do seem to respond cyclically to the economy's patterns. These, therefore, can be bought or sold within a business-cycle framework, if there is a reasonable degree of assurance that there will be no unpleasant political surprises.

Let's consider first a tangible that shares many of gold's characteristics—silver. Like gold, silver is rare, durable, and can be easily made into coins. Thus it can perform two important monetary functions—it can serve as a medium of exchange and as a store of value. It's no coincidence that the price of silver over the centuries has tended to move within a ratio of approximately $15 per unit of gold to $1.00 per unit of silver. History makes clear that periodic attempts to replace silver—or gold—as a monetary standard have eventually failed. Like gold, silver has proved a particularly sound investment in times of prolonged, severe inflation.

But what can be said about silver's relationship to the relatively short-term ups and downs of the economy? Nearly 75 percent of all newly mined silver is found in conjunction with other so-called base metals, such as copper, nickel, lead, or zinc. Like those metals, silver production usually fluctuates in response to changes in the business cycle. In down-phases of the cycle, production of base metals generally slumps along with declining industrial activity and demand. When that happens, mine production of silver also tends to drop. This reduction in silver output, of course, tends to bolster the metal's price in recessionary times. However, experience shows that the drop in output—and therefore in supply—has proved insufficient to eliminate any reduction in silver prices during periods of declining economic activity. Silver prices do tend to decline ultimately as recessions deepen, and they tend to remain relatively depressed for a considerable while after the economy enters a cyclical up-phase. By the same token, once silver prices begin climbing in an economic upturn, they tend to keep right on moving up for a considerable time after a new recession comes along. This tendency is reinforced by the fact that base metals output—and therefore silver output—is apt to drop rather abruptly once a recession begins.

The upshot is that silver, like gold, normally lags behind the ups and downs of the business cycle. The time to buy is perhaps a year or so after the end of a recession. And the time to sell is perhaps three months or so after a recession has begun. In late 1973, for example, just as the long, severe 1973–75 slump was beginning, silver sold at about $3.00 an ounce. More than three months later, in the spring of 1974, with the recession well under way, the metal's price exceeded $5.00 an ounce. A sustained decline finally began in the early summer of 1974, and it continued right through March of 1975, when a new business-cycle upturn began. A final low point, at $4.00 an ounce, wasn't reached until early 1976, a year after the recession ended. The subsequent rise in prices was gradual at first, but became steep in 1978. By then the new economic up-phase was in full swing, and in addition inflationary pressures were building rapidly, so that traditional inflation hedges such as silver were in high demand for reasons quite apart from business-cycle factors. By the time the 1980 recession began in January of that year, the metal was selling at some $30.00 an ounce. Its price continued to rise in the early stages of the 1980 recession, approaching the $50 level in mid-January 1980 before plummeting in March. The relatively short recession ended in the summer of 1980, with silver selling at about $17 an ounce. However, as late as February 1981, a half year into the next recovery phase of the business cycle, silver was selling at only about $12 an ounce.

As the movement of silver and gold prices indicates, the prices of many tangibles tend to lag behind the ups and downs of the economy as a whole.

However, few items so clearly behave as lagging indicators. Very generally, prices of base metals such as copper also follow a less pronounced lagging pattern. Copper prices, for instance, kept rising, like gold and silver prices, through the early months of the 1973–75 recession and were about as low two years afterward as they were when that recession ended in March of 1975. A distinction is apparent, however. The copper price level, while tending to lag behind the business cycle, doesn't lag as greatly as, say, gold and silver price levels. The explanation no doubt is that industrial demand plays a far greater role in the copper business than it does in the silver or, especially, gold business. Thus, a slowdown in general economic activity tends to be reflected relatively rapidly in the copper market. The sort of investment interest that bolsters demand for gold and silver, especially around business-cycle peaks when inflation may be severe, simply isn't a major factor where copper is concerned.

Other metals whose price behavior tends to lag behind the business cycle range from steel scrap to aluminum. A wide variety of still other metals is available to investors, and generally it may be said that their price behavior, within a business-cycle framework, has tended to follow that of the better-known metals. Among these other metals are the following:

Antimony, used in auto batteries, flame retardants, medicines, pigments, and matches; bismuth, used in pharmaceuticals and chemicals; cadmium, used in pigments, electroplating, and low-melting alloys; chromium, used in stainless steel, high-strength alloys, and chrome-plate; cobalt, used in cathodes, jet-engine alloys, paint compounds, and varnishes; germanium, used in electronics; indium, used in alloys, soldering, and coatings; iridium, used in alloys, pen tips, and compass bearings; manganese, used in making steel, flash bulbs, and incendiary bombs; mercury, used in chlorine, caustic soda, and electrical-contact production; molybdenum, used in making steel and chemicals; rhodium, used in jewelry, mirrors, and as an alloy with platinum in aircraft; selenium, used in electronics, photocopying, and glass insulation; tellurium, used in thermal electronics, chemicals, rubber, and ceramics; vanadium, used in making steel.

Investing in such relatively obscure items isn't as difficult as you may think. Brokerage houses can make such purchases for you. Bache Halsey Stuart Shield Inc., for example, will trade minor metals for retail accounts, as well as for large commercial accounts. A Bache official stresses that "international politics can affect metals which are primarily dependent on one country, or several countries, which follow a single political ideology. For example, the prime source for cobalt, especially in its purest forms, is Zaire. This central African country has gone from colonial status as the Belgian Congo to worldwide recognition during its struggle for political independence." The Bache analyst goes on to warn that "South Africa is also a supplier of many minor metals and has been subject to various political strife and the impact of sympathetic embargo. Manganese is chiefly supplied by Russia. Mercury comes from both sides of the globe, with Spain and China as two key sources; one of the main sources for chromium is Turkey." The advice here is generally to avoid such esoteric investment dealings, particularly in light of the political uncertainties involved. However, you should know that even such obscure tangibles are available for purchase, if you're determined to plunge into such risky investment areas.

Returning to more conventional tangible investments, we should stress that it would be a large mistake to assume that all tangibles follow the sort of price pattern apparent in most metals. A case in point is lumber. It would seem that the home-building industry tends to behave as a leading economic indicator. It's no surprise, therefore, to observe that lumber prices also tend to move up or down ahead of the business cycle. For instance, lumber prices reached a peak in early 1973, more than half a year before the 1973–75 recession began. In sharp contrast to gold, silver, or copper prices, the price of lumber had been falling sharply for many months when the recession actually started in November 1973. Conversely, lumber prices hit a recessionary bottom in the fall of 1974 and had been climbing sharply for about six months when the 1973–75 recession ended. The climb continued, it should be noted, for almost precisely five years, with little interruption until the fall of 1979. Then a steep decline set in. The decline was full blown by the time the 1980 recession began in January of that year. Again, this represents a very different pattern from the sort of behavior of many tangibles.

On the Farm

Up to now in this chapter, we've concentrated on tangibles that generally are dug from deep in the ground or, as in the case of lumber, cut from deep in the forest. There's another broad area of tangibles, however, that requires discussion—agricultural products. These, too, can provide an investment vehicle for the prudent do-it-yourselfer. But we must warn that successful investing here will require a degree of expertise that extends far beyond an understanding of just the business cycle. Indeed, other sorts of cycles get involved, and you may well find that learning about them is simply too time-consuming. Even more than in the case of, say, lumber, prices of farm items may move up or down in response to factors that have little or no connection to the ups and downs of the economy. Indeed, if you wish to become involved in agricultural investing, you'll find that you must begin by studying a whole new variety of cycles that don't appear, for example, in *Business Conditions Digest*.

There is, for instance, something called the "cattle cycle." Any relationship between it and the business cycle that we know is largely coincidental. The population of cattle in the United States swells and shrinks in a predictable pattern. The cycle starts when the supply of beef is tight and, accordingly, beef prices are at relatively lofty levels. To take advantage of the price situation, cattle ranchers will attempt, pardon the pun, to beef up their herds by holding on to young females to use them for breeding instead of for slaughter. Then, in a few years, the supply of beef will grow plentiful as a result of this policy, and naturally beef prices will tend to decline. Then ranchers will sell their breeding stocks to trim their losses. Subsequently, the beef price level will begin to firm and rise again, and the cycle repeats itself. The entire evolution stretches across a decade or more, which, as we've seen, is a good deal longer time than the typical expansion-recession-recovery pattern of the business cycle.

If you wish to engage in cattle trading, you obviously will have to familiarize yourself with the cattle cycle. You'll have to be able to understand it and to grasp where matters stand at a particular moment. In this regard, take warning from a study published by New York's Citibank in November 1979 that traces the price of steers at Omaha over two decades. In the process, it notes the ups and downs of steer prices in relation to the ups and downs of the business cycle. A glance at the study leaves the overriding impression that there is simply no relationship. For example, steer prices were higher at the end of the 1973–75 recession than at its start. The message: If you do want to engage in such investing, which obviously has so little to do with the economy's ups and downs, you would be best advised to begin by studying the cattle cycle. For starters, be aware that cows have one calf each year and that the calf won't be ready for market until it's almost two years old. The longest cattle cycle on record lasted sixteen years, ending in 1928. The first fully measured cattle cycle began at a beef-producing lull all the way back in 1896. Since that cycle, there have been seven others, averaging a dozen years in duration, with seven years of expansion, on the average, and five years of contraction. According to a 1979 study by the Chicago Federal Reserve Bank, during the expansion phases cattle numbers rose an average of 28 percent and, during the contraction phases, the average decline was 12 percent.

To place all this into a sort of farmland perspective, other animals exhibit other cyclical patterns, and these depend on such concerns as varying gestation periods. For instance, a sow can produce two litters of eight to ten piglets each year, and they are ready for market in less than six months. A hen serves in the hatchery about ten months a year, producing around 150 eggs. The eggs hatch after three weeks in an incubator.

Other agricultural items—all under the broad heading of investment tangibles—range from corn to soybeans to cocoa to wheat to cotton to sugar. All these, and others, can be bought or sold through the commodities department of major brokerage houses, and such purchases, through the use of credit, can be highly leveraged, so that a relatively modest amount of cash can, if you guess right, produce fat profits. But the emphasis here must be on the word "guess." As the complexity of the cattle cycle suggests, this sort of investing signifies a whole new, and much riskier, ballgame for the do-it-yourselfer. The Wall Street area to be sure, is replete with commodities experts who can tell you all about the hog cycle or the cattle cycle. And they may occasionally really know what they are talking about. But if you listen and then heed their advice, you will no longer be doing it yourself. You won't be your own investment adviser. So, unless you really have the time to delve into such arcane matters as the gestation period of pigs, or how weather patterns in Ghana are affecting cocoa-bean growth, your best bet is to stick to investments that are linked directly to something that can readily be monitored—the business cycle.

Collectibles

A brief mention should be made about a very special sort of tangible—the so-called collectible. As we've seen, tangibles cover a wide assortment of items, large and small, animate and inanimate, costly and cheap. Collectibles are tangibles, usually available through auctions and the like, whose value has little direct connection with the business cycle, but rather rests on the degree of preciousness, rarity involved, and fashion of the particular period. Many collectibles are readily recognizable, such as antique furniture, diamonds, rare books, china, paintings, and prints. Others can be most unusual—old comic books, lead soldiers made years ago, baseball cards, and so on. But all collectibles have a common denominator in that they tend to grow costlier when inflation worsens over the long term. This secular trend, quite obviously, transcends the ups and downs of the business cycle. If you decide that inflation will keep on worsening and you happen to enjoy collecting, say, lead soldiers, the chances are, if you know your soldiers, you'll be making a reasonably sound investment. But if you don't know or appreciate lead soldiers, skip the whole idea. Stick to the stock market or the bond market or even that Omaha beef if you know something about the cattle cycle. One study shows, for example, that in a five-year period of painful inflation, the price of a Mickey Mouse film projector rose from $45 to $175, of a pair of Civil War binoculars from $20 to $50, and of an 1880 wicker baby carriage with iron wheels from $125 to $325. There aren't many experts on 1880 baby carriages.

Whether one is dealing in collectibles or other tangibles, it must again be stressed that a relatively high degree of investor risk obtains.

American Institute Counselors, Inc., the Great Barrington, Massachusetts, investment advisory service founded by the late Colonel Edward C. Harwood (see Chapter 5), warns investors planning to enter the market for rare collectibles, for example, to be prepared to "accept significant risks. Even after the market value of a rare stamp or rare photograph has been determined through auction bidding or fixed dealer's prices, the purchase cost often is inflated by as much as 20% to 30%." These expenses include finder's fees, dealer commissions, and auction house commissions, the report notes. Regarding trading of commodities, John Train, a columnist for *Forbes* magazine, has written: "The one true and obvious reason why commodity speculators lose money is . . . that the retail commodity speculator does not belong in the market at all. If he keeps going long enough, he's almost sure to lose his money, just as though he was playing the slots at Las Vegas. He is a sucker, a victim, not a client to the industry."

If you must trade in tangibles, such as agricultural products, try to do so through a reputable brokerage firm and use what brokers call "stop-loss orders" to safeguard your investment against sustaining severe losses. These orders instruct your broker to offset your position, once prices have reached a specified adverse level. About thirty-five commodities have active markets, and information on all of them is available through reputable brokerage houses.

15.
Putting
It
Together

MEET SAM SAGACIOUS. HE'S A MYTHICAL FELLOW I'VE CREATED who long has been practicing the investment technique preached on these pages. He knows all about the business cycle, with its up-phases and its down-phases. He can spot a recession a mile off. He knows the difference between a leading indicator and a lagging indicator. He reads *Business Conditions Digest* religiously each month. He knows when various key economic statistics appear each month in his favorite newspaper—*The Wall Street Journal*, of course—and he knows just where in the paper to look for them. For instance, on Friday, October 30, 1981, he knew that the Commerce Department's report on its three composite indexes—the leading, coincident, and lagging indicators—would appear that morning in *The Wall Street Journal*. He knew that it would probably appear in a major news article at the top of page three, where the paper's editors normally place important "spot" news stories each day. He was right. Far down in the story, Sam even located the latest reading for the early-early warning ratio of coincident-to-lagging indicators. A brief outline of the article, in addition, appeared on the paper's front page, in the second column from the left, in a section headlined "WHAT'S

NEWS—," which summarized most of the day's most important stories and informed readers where in the paper various major pieces appeared.

The *Journal* story on the indicators gave Sam much of the information that he felt was necessary for setting his investment plans. It not only reported the movement in September of the three composite indexes and the ratio, but also traced the behavior of his favorite individual barometers, all components of the leading-indicator composite—building permits, the inflation-adjusted money supply, and the stock market as measured by the Standard & Poor's index of 500 common stocks. The ups and downs of this index, of course, are reported daily in the financial press, but Sam preferred following only the monthly trend on the theory that focusing on the market's daily gyrations was too confusing and, in any event, cut too deeply into his fishing and golfing activities.

Sam Sagacious could afford to golf and fish to his heart's content in October of 1981 because he had managed over the last dozen years, despite all the economy's problems, to build himself a tidy nest egg. He did this primarily in the turbulent decade of 1968–78, an interval spanning two recessions, the latter of which lasted nearly a year and a half and was by far the severest setback that the U.S. economy had encountered to that time since the Great Depression in the 1930s. In the 1973–75 business downturn, the nation's jobless rate nearly reached double-digit readings. Let's take a closer look at how Sam invested his money during that ten years, and how he came to his portfolio decisions.

His individual moves weren't always successful, as we will see. But they were successful enough to put Sam far along the road to the financial independence that he enjoyed in October of 1981. A cautious man by nature, Sam eschewed many of the investment vehicles mentioned in earlier chapters. Although he owned a few gold coins—mostly double eagles left him by his late mother—he otherwise refrained from plowing money into tangibles. While he appreciated their relationship to the ups and downs of the business cycle, he felt that the link was a bit too tenuous to suit his cautious nature. For similar reasons, he restricted his investing in fixed-income securities to short-term instruments, mainly in the form of Treasury bills, which he bought through a stockbroker. Mindful of the importance of long-term trends that transcend the familiar business cycle, Sam had determined in the mid-1960s that inflation, particularly with Uncle Sam's increasing military involvement in Vietnam, would tend slowly to intensify from one business-cycle sequence to the next. Considering such a secular pattern, he concluded that fixed-income securities, especially those having a long-term maturity, were a bit too risky for his delicate stomach. He would sleep better with the bulk of his money in the stock market where, as we've noted, dividend yields aren't fixed but will tend to rise or fall according to changes in the economic climate. However, with inflation again in mind, he would shun public-utility stocks.

How It Began

It all began, according to Sam, in the spring of 1968 when his Aunt Millie unexpectedly died and left her life savings of $16,475 to Sam, her favorite nephew. Sam recalls that at the time of her death, on May 14, 1968, the Standard & Poor's index of 500 stocks stood at 98.12, or almost precisely where the same S&P index stood—at 98.76—ten years later, on May 15, 1978.

Over the course of that ten years, then, the S&P index barely budged. But Sam Sagacious' portfolio budged, all right. Upon Aunt Millie's death, he promptly bought with his inheritance 200 shares of General Motors common stock, selling on May 14, 1968, at $82.375 a share, or $16,475 for the full amount. Why General Motors?

As a student of the business cycle, Sam was well aware in May 1968 that the economy had been enjoying a cyclical up-phase for a long, long time. He knew that the National Bureau of Economic Research, which in those days was based in New York City rather than Cambridge, Massachusetts, had determined long ago that the 1960–61 recession had ended early in 1961—in February of that year to be precise. And he knew that nothing had happened since then, despite a few rough patches, to derail the upturn. In May 1968 it was already the longest up-phase of the cycle in U.S. history. Sam knew all this. But he also knew that important indicators of future economic activity were still flashing green. As he thumbed through his latest issue of BCD, he noted that the leading-indicator index was, in fact, in a strong uptrend. The latest reading available to him when his aunt died was for March 1968, because of Commerce Department reporting lags and the time it took for his mail subscription to BCD to reach him. In March, he noted, the leading-indicator index stood at 104.8. He further observed in BCD that the barometer had been rising almost steadily, month after month, since January 1967, when it stood at 95.6.

Some of the other indicators that Sam knew to be particularly useful for investment decisions, were not, unfortunately, printed in BCD in those days, although they all are nowadays. Accordingly, he had to work a few statistics out for himself each month, like the inflation-adjusted money supply and the ratio of coincident-to-lagging indicators; the two individual composite indexes were contained in BCD, but Sam had to perform the division—the numerator was the coincident index, the denominator the lagging index—to obtain the ratio. Other key indicators, such as the Standard & Poor's stock index and the building-permit series, were carried then, as now, in the publication. (In those early years, Sam was too poor to buy *The Wall Street Journal* regularly, even though it was much cheaper and thinner then than now, so he often had to wait for his BCD issue to find the latest reading on one or another indicator.)

In May 1968 he observed, after performing the necessary arithmetic, that the ratio of coincident-to-lagging indicators, at 102.4, was at its highest level in two years. He also noted that building permits and the real money supply had both been rising briskly since late 1966.

Assessing such data, Sam readily concluded that the economic expansion period that had begun all the way back in February 1961 still had ways to go. He further knew from his business-cycle research that the fortunes of companies producing and selling consumer goods normally rise and fall in approximate unison with the business cycle. General Motors, with its focus on automotive products, trucks, and home appliances, impressed him as such a consumer-oriented company. Its size and longevity also attracted him. Sticking to large, proven corporations was an important part of his investing technique. He could relax more with his money invested in companies, such as General Motors, that were clearly recognized as leaders of their industries.

The First Switch

Sam held onto his 200 shares until June 16, 1969, slightly more than a year. Then he sold all of them at $78.50 a share, taking a loss on his initial stake of $16,475. On the same day, he bought 178 shares of Ingersoll-Rand at about $44 a share, for a total cost of $7,850. He held the other $7,850—the other half of his proceeds from his sale of General Motors—in the form of cold cash.

Why did he decide to sell his General Motors? Why did he put the proceeds evenly into Ingersoll-Rand and cash?

The answers, once again, can be found in what Sam observed in his latest issue of BCD. He saw, first off, that the leading-indicator index no longer was rising briskly. Instead, it had begun to wobble nervously. At 111.4 in April 1969, the latest month recorded in his new issue of BCD, the index was up slightly from the March level. But it was well below readings as far back as December and January. Clearly, the sustained climb, evident when he purchased the General Motors shares just over a year earlier, was at an end. Still more significant to Sam was the fact, which he deduced from other data in the issue, that the ratio of coincident-to-lagging indicators was actually in a sustained decline. The April reading of 99.1 was the lowest since March 1967, more than two years before. The ratio had been falling almost without interruption for six months. The April 1969 reading was down from 102.8 as recently as November 1968. This behavior stood as a clear warning to Sam that the long economic expansion might soon be running out of gas. He was keenly aware, as a student of business-cycle patterns, that the ratio was an especially early precursor of economic things to come. Sam also saw in June 1969 that the stock market itself was wobbling somewhat. He knew, of course, that the Standard & Poor's index of 500 common stocks was a reliable, particularly farseeing leading indicator. He noted in his latest issue of BCD that the stock-market gauge actually stood slightly below its early-1969 level. It had risen sharply in late 1968, he noticed, but then fallen abruptly for a few months, before bouncing back a bit in the spring of 1969. He concluded that the stock market's performance suggested at the least a need for a cautious investment stance.

Putting the various statistical developments together, Sam decided that the expansion phase of the cycle wasn't over yet; the leading-indicator index was only wobbling, not falling persistently and sharply in the sort of pattern that typically develops in the very last stages of an economic up-phase. But Sam also was convinced from the data that the expansion was becoming exceedingly long in the tooth. Being ultracautious, he decided in June 1969 to sell his General Motors stock and put half the proceeds straight into cash, just in case the recession actually was at hand. Taking the tiniest of gambles with the other half of his money, he opted to buy into an industry that traditionally is slow to slip when a recession begins (just as it is slow to recover when a recovery arrives).

Choosing a Leader

One such industry, he was aware from his familiarity with business-cycle history, was the capital-equipment business. Ingersoll-Rand, he knew, was the world's largest producer of compressors and such related machinery as rock drills, hoists, and air-operated tools. Its other products ranged from coal-mining and pulp-processing machinery to construction equipment. Clearly, it met his conservative requirement that he restrict his stock buying to well-established industry leaders. He also noted that the Value Line Investment Survey, which the business section of his community library subscribed to each week, had given Ingersoll-Rand stock its number-one rating for "safety." (The Value Line investment advisory service covers scores of important stocks over the course of a year, focusing on different industries each week, and rates the relative safety of each stock on a basis of one, for most safe, to five, for most risky.)

Sam knew that he would have to sell his Ingersoll-Rand once it was evident that a recession was well along. Such capital-equipment stocks, while they traditionally resist recessionary weakness in the early months of a slump, eventually come tumbling down in slumps, along with other types of securities. By April 15, 1970, Sam decided that that time had come. He sold his Ingersoll-Rand shares at about $42.125 a share, slightly under what he had paid for the stock back in June 1969. He conservatively put the proceeds of the sale—$7,498—into cash, giving him a cash total of $15,348. The signals that helped to convince him that a recession was firmly entrenched included pronounced, persistent declines in both the leading-indicator index and the ratio of coincident-to-lagging indicators and a sharply falling Standard & Poor's index. In addition, he observed a somber new development. Indexes that reflect current rather than future economic activity were also beginning to fall unmistakably. Industrial production had been dropping since late 1969. The coincident-indicator index itself was also starting to fall; its components, besides industrial production, include such broad-gauge measures of current business conditions as employment and inflation-adjusted personal income and business sales. To clinch the matter, Sam observed that the unemployment rate had begun climbing. He knew that the jobless rate was an unreliable indicator of economic conditions—except to confirm the severity of a recession once one was solidly in place.

Anticipating the end of a recession, Sam was aware, was somewhat trickier than spotting the approach of one. So, as he sat with his cash, he tried to pay somewhat closer attention to his monthly *BCD* copies, as well as to the occasional issues of *The Wall Street Journal* that he could afford. The $16,475 that Aunt Millie had left him was down to $15,348 now, a loss on capital of more than $1,000. But he had such faith in his technique of investing by way of the business cycle that the loss didn't disturb him in the slightest. He was certain that if he stuck by his guns he would come out a winner. (His loss was really slightly less than it appears, because the numbers presented, while neglecting brokerage fees, also don't take into account the dividend payments that Sam received on his stocks or the modest interest payments that his cash yielded from the savings bank where he kept it in a day-of-deposit to day-of-withdrawal account.)

Playing the Upturn

By September of 1970 Sam began to suspect that a business-cycle upturn was forming just over the horizon. Several factors led him to this suspicion. First, the leading-indicator index was no longer dropping sharply. It had flattened out of late. For a full six months, he noted, the index had held within a fraction of a percentage point to the 104 level. Moreover, the extra-early warning ratio of coincident-to-lagging indicators had risen slightly in July, the latest month available to Sam. This alone wouldn't have prompted him to make an investment change. But two other particularly farseeing indicators were rising with vigor—the building-permit series, which had been surging in recent months, and the money-supply series. The clear strength of these indicators convinced him to make a change, even though some widely publicized other gauges showed that the economy was still in the grip of a recession. For instance, industrial production was still falling and the unemployment rate was still rising sharply.

Following his business-cycle technique, Sam opted to buy into an industry that normally recovers ahead of the economy in general. Housing, he knew, was just such an industry. The recent surge in building permits strengthened his conviction that he should buy a home-building stock. He settled on U. S. Home, once again conservatively selecting an industry leader. It ranked as the largest U.S. builder of single-family housing and was deeply involved in the burgeoning retirement-community market. On September 14, 1970, accordingly, he used his $15,348 to buy 527 shares of U. S. Home at just over $29 a share. In mid-1972, the shares were split two-for-one by the U. S. Home board of directors, so that Sam wound up with 1,054 shares.

Once the economy really had moved from a recession into a firmly established expansion, Sam knew that it would be time to sell his housing-industry shares and move his money into some consumer-oriented company whose fortunes tended to ride along with the economic mainstream. He knew that home-building shares tended to lag once an expansion period neared its mature stages. He decided, therefore, in January 1972, that such a business-cycle stage had arrived. The various early-warning indicators that he followed were generally still on the rise at that time. But so finally was the coincident-indicator index. Its key component, industrial production, had been on the increase with little interruption for nearly a year. In sum, all systems appeared go. The expansion was no longer a fledgling upturn but a mature, full-blown growth period.

Making his move, Sam sold his 1,054 U. S. Home shares on January 13, 1972, at just under $24 a share, for a total of

$25,164. He put the money into the quintessential consumer-goods company, Sears, Roebuck & Co., the world's largest retailer of general merchandise, a firm rated number one in safety by Value Line. His money bought him 251 Sears shares, at just over $100 a share. Now he would sit back and wait for a signal that the expansion was losing its steam.

That signal didn't come for a full year. Then, on January 15, 1973, Sam sold his 251 Sears shares at about $117.25 a share. He put half of the total proceeds of $29,430 into cash and half into his old friend Ingersoll-Rand. The $14,715 he used for the stock purchase gained him 212 shares of Ingersoll-Rand at a price of just over $69 a share. His decision reflected several factors. The leading-indicator index was still on the rise. But the ratio of coincident-to-lagging indicators appeared to be beginning to wobble, up one month, down another, up the next. Moreover, building permits had declined in September, October, and November of 1972, the latest month carried in *BCD*. If the expansion were indeed starting to lose vigor, the Ingersoll-Rand shares should hold up well as the next cyclical down-phase developed. And the cash provided an extra measure of safety in case a recession came on faster and harder than Sam estimated.

A year later there was no question in Sam's mind that a major recession was settled in. The leading-indicator index had been dropping fairly steadily since March 1973. The ratio had been on the decline for almost a full year. Building permits had been falling like a stone for about the same amount of time. The share-price and money-supply gauges also showed persistent falloffs. Industrial production looked wobbly. The unemployment rate was still relatively low, but no longer declining as it had been in much of 1973. Sam was impressed by the speed with which the lagging-indicator index was climbing. This composite index, the denominator of his favorite ratio, was composed of individual economic gauges that tend, when they rise extrasteeply, to inhibit further business growth and possibly bring on a recession. They include such facets of the economic scene as labor costs per unit of output, the ratio of consumer installment credit to personal income, the average bank prime rate, inflation-adjusted business inventories, and commercial and industrial loans outstanding at large commercial banks.

The big climb in the lagging indicators was the final straw. Sam sold his 212 shares of Ingersoll-Rand at $89.50 a share on January 14, 1974. Adding the $18,974 proceeds from the sale to his $14,715 already held in cash, he now had a considerable nest egg, all in cash, of $33,689. He would now ride out the recession.

Slightly more than a year later, on February 14, 1975, Sam decided that the long 1973–75 recession was finally approaching an end. Accordingly, reverting to a recovery-time strategy that he had used before, he put the entire $33,689 into U. S. Home stock. The recession had hit the home-building business, along with many other businesses, very hard. As a result, the stock was selling at only $4.375 a share. Sam, therefore, was able to buy 7,700 shares. His estimate that the recession was nearing an end reflected his observation that three key barometers had stopped falling—the money-supply gauge, building permits, and the S&P stock index. Moreover, the lagging-indicator composite had stopped rising and was starting to ease down. Such key coincident indicators as industrial production were still dropping hard and the jobless rate was soaring. But Sam's familiarity with business-cycle trends told him that unemployment usually did climb extra-sharply as a recession ended and even often in the early months of a new up-phase of the cycle. The recession would soon end, he concluded, before picking up the phone to order 7,700 shares of U. S. Home stock.

As late as May 15, 1978, Sam still had his 7,700 U. S. Home shares. At $9.25 each, the shares—and Sam—were worth on that day $71,225, or more than 4.3 times what Aunt Millie had left. He not only had managed to enlarge this inheritance, but he did so over ten years in which the overall stock market, gauged in terms of the Standard & Poor's 500 stock index went precisely nowhere. And he achieved his success without gambling his money on little-known stocks that might—or might not—strike it rich. Indeed, he limited his stock-picking in all instances to stocks representing well-established industry leaders. Aunt Millie would have been proud.

16.
Loose
Ends

THROUGHOUT THIS GUIDE TO AN INVESTMENT STRATEGY THAT you can reasonably undertake on your own, in good times or bad, an underlying theme has been simplicity. Stick to basics. Learn the rhythms of the business cycle and how this cyclical behavior tends to influence the major investment categories—stocks, bonds, key tangibles. Apply the strategy, in good times or bad, through inflationary periods or periods of relatively stable prices. A further point has been made and repeated—to eschew, unless you are willing to assume a full-time project, a myriad of relatively arcane investment techniques and channels. The strategy this book has provided, in brief, constitutes a layman's guide, intended for those who can only devote a limited number of hours each week to building and preserving savings.

Even in such a strategy, however, loose ends emerge that must be tied. Questions arise that have little or no direct bearing on, say, whether capital-goods spending tends to lead, coincide with, or lag behind the ups and downs of the economy as a whole. Short of struggling through the entire esoteric lexicon of investing, how can the layman best master some of

LOOSE ENDS

the key words and phrases that are useful in grasping the business-cycle picture? Again shying away from an endless procession of available literature, how can the layman select the reading that seems most appropriate, given the layman's time constraints? Apart from the vast intricacy of tax regulations, what aspects of taxation may pertain particularly in an investment strategy geared, as this one must be, to the business cycle? Quite obviously, definitive answers are impossible to come by. However, reasonable suggestions, drawn from personal experience, can readily be supplied.

Here, to begin, are a few of the terms that are likely to arise in do-it-yourself investing geared to the business cycle. A few, drawn from earlier chapters, will be familiar to you. Others may not be.

We've talked again and again about the *business cycle*, and we've described its dimensions in a variety of ways. But a thumbnail definition may still be in order. Essentially, the business cycle is the repetitive process of expansion and contraction periods that has characterized the economy's progress since pre-Civil War years, when the record keeping started. The up-phases of the cycle culminate in what economists call *peaks* and the down-phases in *troughs*. The time from peak to trough is referred to by economists as a *contraction period* and the time from trough to peak as an *expansion period*. In popular jargon, contraction periods have come to be known, usually, as *recessions* and expansion periods, up to a point, as *recoveries*. Recessions that go on for very long intervals and involve very high levels of joblessness—with unemployment rates extending into double-digit territory—are popularly called *depressions*. However, for business-cycle analysis, depressions and recessions are all lumped together as contractions. Similarly, recoveries that extend over long periods and witness new high levels of overall economic activity, surpassing pre-recessionary levels, are referred to as expansions, on the theory that business is no longer simply recovering from a previous contraction. Again, economists apply the term "expansion" to any part of a trough-to-peak period, whether it appears to be simply a recovery situation or something far more solid.

A word more about peaks and troughs. They are designated, as we have seen earlier, by the month. A contraction period, for instance, doesn't begin on a particular day. It begins—and for that matter it ends—during a particular month. The same can be said of an expansion. For practical purposes, midmonth is usually taken to be the cyclical turning point, whether a peak or a trough is involved. Thus, if we say that a recession reached its trough in March 1975, as in fact one did, that month becomes both the final month of a contraction and the first month of a subsequent expansion. Think of the first half of that month in 1975 as a part of the 1973–75 recession and the second half as a part of the 1975–80 expansion.

While we're defining the business cycle, you should bear in mind that all sorts of other cycles exist, from the awesome—but possibly fictional—Kondratieff wave cycle to the far less romantic cattle and hog cycles. Please don't confuse any of these other cycles with the central business cycle that has been the focus of this book. That cycle and not these others provides the investment framework within which the do-it-yourself investor must operate. But be aware that other cycles exist as well, and that they also occasionally can affect investments.

Turning to the indicators of the cycle, we've discussed at some length the various sorts of economic yardsticks—leading, coincident, and lagging. Knowing the key components of each category is crucial to a successful do-it-yourself investment strategy. Remember that leading indicators tend to move up, down, or sideways in advance of the economy as a whole. Coincident indicators tend to move concurrently with the broad business trend. And lagging indicators, as the name implies, tend to lag behind the business cycle's ups and downs. Know the patterns, know the indicators, and then invest accordingly.

There are a few other indicators, not mentioned in earlier chapters, that can be useful to the do-it-yourselfer. Data worth your attempting to keep tabs on include, for instance, the so-called Duncan indicator, a sort of leading indicator that combines various sales statistics in a manner that over many years has produced a remarkably farseeing guide to the business cycle's ups and downs. There is also a leading indicator index devised by the Center for International Business Cycle Research of Rutgers University, in Newark, New Jersey. This yardstick, focusing on a variety of labor-force data, is of more recent vintage. However, in its brief existence, it has proved to be a reliable precursor of such trends as unemployment. The Rutgers Center is directed by Geoffrey Moore, a former U.S. Commissioner of Labor Statistics and a leading authority on business-cycle history. Its useful statistics also include a batch of leading-indicator indexes for foreign countries—at last count, the six major industrial nations of the West. Less accurate and less timely than, for example, the Commerce Department's well-known leading-indicator index, these six barometers are nonetheless helpful for do-it-yourself investing, particularly if foreign investments kindle any interest. The data are available through the Conference Board, a nonprofit research organization based in New York City.

Where to Turn

Let me suggest a few places to turn if you wish—despite my warnings to keep things simple—to broaden your familiarity with the esoterica of financial jargon. The New York Stock Exchange has published a marvelous little booklet, appropriately titled *Glossary—The Language of Investing*. Therein you will find concise and accurate definitions of all the sorts of things I have skimmed over or avoided entirely in this book —puts and calls, odd lots, margin calls, upticks, downticks, arbitrage, hypothecation, and on and on and on. The New York Stock Exchange, with a large and capable public information staff, will make this booklet available, I am informed, to anyone taking the trouble to contact it at its Wall Street headquarters.

What else might one read? We've already shown the crucial importance of the Commerce Department's *Business Conditions Digest*. But what else? The supply of investment literature is seemingly endless, and no effort will be made here to list more than a fraction of the available material. However, a discriminating attempt can be undertaken, first, to point out some publications that, like *BCD*, should help you to gain a fuller appreciation of the business cycle and cycles generally. Such material, surprisingly, isn't all that abundant. A thorough discussion of the business cycle—perhaps more thorough than you may want to digest, but still a valuable reference—is *Business Cycle Indicators*, edited by Geoffrey H. Moore and published by Princeton University Press in 1961. The first, fatter, volume of the two-volume work contains an assortment of analyses of the behavior of the business cycle; the second, relatively thin, volume is largely statistical. Another worthwhile study of the business cycle, much shorter and simpler, is *Indicators of Business Expansions and Contractions*, by Geoffrey Moore and the late Julius Shiskin, who, like Mr. Moore, was a former U.S. Commissioner of Labor Statistics; it was published in 1967 by the Columbia University Press for the National Bureau of Economic Research. This slender book rates various economic indicators according to such standards as timing, currency, and significance. It also contains a variety of charts depicting the precise patterns of key indicators in terms of expansion and contraction phases. Here, for instance, you would see clearly the relationship between building permits and the onset of recessions—information that could prove highly beneficial, as we have seen, if you plan to put money into home-building securities.

Still another book that helps broaden one's understanding of the business cycle is a volume of collected essays by Arthur F. Burns, former chairman of the Federal Reserve Board, entitled *The Business Cycle in a Changing World*; it was published in 1969 by the National Bureau of Economic Research and distributed by the Columbia University Press. Mr. Burns writes clearly and concisely, and you don't need to have a degree in economics to understand his points about the economy's ups and downs and their wide-ranging ramifications.

Two other works are worth perusing, even though neither deals directly with the conventional, familiar business cycle that should be the focus of the do-it-yourself investor. One is *Cycles*, by Dick A. Stoken, published by McGraw-Hill in 1978. The author, who has a business background, discusses in a somewhat technical fashion a variety of cycles, real or imagined, that generally transcend the standard business cycle. Mr. Stoken's book is valuable because it focuses on ways to profit from investment cycles. His background enables him to be particularly helpful with regard to commodity investing which, as we've seen, can be a hazardous undertaking.

The Kondratieff Wave, by James B. Shuman and David Rosenau and published by World Publishing in 1972, is a detailed look at the famous long-term cycle discussed in Chapter 7. Mr. Shuman's background as a journalist, with *Reader's Digest* among other publications, helps explain the book's readability. Mr. Rosenau's background as an investment banker in New York provides a useful element of business expertise. While I remain a good deal more skeptical than the authors appear to be about the existence of any such supercycle, their book gives the layman an additional degree of perspective in assessing the economy's cyclical nature and how that nature can influence investments.

Moving beyond the business cycle, the assortment of reading material available to the do-it-yourself investor is considerable. Spending vast amounts of time trying to wade through all of it would be impossible. But a sampling of the best available material from a broad cross section may be helpful. For starters, a subscription to *The Wall Street Journal*, the national business daily, is a must. Published therein, Monday through Friday, are virtually all of the economic statistics that the do-it-yourself investor must follow, at least occasionally, in order to stay ahead of the ups and downs of the business cycle. Late each month the *Journal* carries in considerable detail the Commerce Department's leading-indicator report, along with its composite indexes of coincident and lagging indicators, as well as the farseeing ratio of the coincident-to-lagging indicators explained in Chapter 9. In addition, the *Journal* regularly reports on such matters as monthly changes in housing starts, building permits, and machine tool orders; weekly data on the fluctuations in the money supply in all its various forms; the daily movements of share prices; monthly changes in various price indexes, from consumer to wholesale level; quarterly data on profits, profit margins, and the gross national product; plus countless other statistics that relate, closely or remotely, to the business cycle.

Besides the *Journal*, I would also urge a subscription to *Business Week*, the McGraw-Hill weekly magazine that, in my view, provides persistently superior, clearly written reportage on a broad range of business developments, both in the United States and abroad. You can happily skip a lot of the more specialized articles that deal at length with particular subjects that may be far removed from business-cycle matters. However, each week you will also find in *Business Week* a number of regular columns, as well as other articles, that do clearly bear on the economy's ups and downs—reports that will appraise everything from the business-inventory situation in a given week to assessments of future Federal Reserve monetary policy.

Both *The Wall Street Journal* and *Business Week* regularly contain plentiful information about commodity trends. Both publications will also occasionally offer longer features on important commodity trends that may be extremely useful to any do-it-yourself investor bold enough to dabble in that market. For instance, in April 1981 the *Journal* carried on its front page an exhaustive feature report about how rice was supplanting cotton as "king" of commodity crops in various parts of the United States. The *Journal*, I should add, regularly covers the gold market and occasionally carries feature articles on developments that can exert a long-term influence on the yellow metal's price.

There are, of course, a number of other magazines and newspapers that can be highly useful in keeping abreast of the business cycle. These include, in no particular order, the New York *Times, Forbes, Barron's, The Economist* (London), and *Fortune* magazine. If you have the time, and the money, to take on the additional reading, by all means do so. But I must frankly say that with *Business Conditions Digest, The Wall Street Journal,* and *Business Week,* you will really have all the fundamental information required for an intelligent assessment of the ever-changing economic scene.

If you should decide to try keeping updated on a daily basis on the various economic statistics pouring from Washington's number mills—more of a chore than even Sam Sagacious would undertake—you should also know approximately when, in each month, particular reports are released by governmental agencies. The exact date may vary slightly from month to month, but the "Economic Calendar," illustrated here is a typical schedule, based on what happened in October 1981.

A few additional publications are also worth noting. For collectors of collectibles, there is a basic introduction titled, reasonably enough, *Collecting Tomorrow's Collectibles,* by Jeffrey Feinman, published by Collier Books in 1979. The author leads the reader through such sections as "the investment potential of collectibles," "what makes an item valuable," and techniques of "buying and selling." For a more precise knowledge of corporate financial statements, written in clear, understandable prose, there is a booklet, updated periodically, by Merrill Lynch & Co. called *How to Read a Financial Statement.* It does its job admirably, exploring such matters as current assets, current and long-term liabilities, capital stock, capital surplus, accumulated retained earnings, net working capital, current ratio, inventory turnover, book value of securities, interest expense, preferred-dividend coverage, and cash flow

Another informative publication of a general nature is a Federal Reserve Bank of Richmond booklet titled *Instruments of the Money Market.* It tells what the money market is all

Economic Calendar

MONDAY	TUESDAY	WEDNESDAY	THURSDAY	FRIDAY
				2 Unemployment
5 Auto sales	6 Consumer credit	7 Wholesale trade	1 Construction expenditures; Manufacturers' shipments, inventories, and orders	
12	13 Advance retail sales	14 10-day auto sales; Manufacturing and trade: inventories and sales	8	9 Producer price index
19 Capacity utilization; Housing starts; Building permits	20 Personal income and consumption	21 GNP	15	16 Industrial production
26 Treasury budget	27	28 Merchandise trade; Productivity and costs	22 Advance report on durable goods	23 10-day auto sales; CPI; Real earnings
			29 Leading indicators	30 Agricultural prices; Single-family home sales and inventories

about and explains in detail such things as Treasury bills, commercial paper, repurchase agreements, federal funds, Eurodollars, and certificates of deposit. The 148-page booklet may be obtained by anyone; simply write for it to the Federal Reserve Bank of Richmond, Richmond, Virginia 23219. Its popularity is evidenced by the fact that a fifth edition was recently issued.

A useful newsletter regarding money-market funds is *Money Market Fund Safety Ratings*, published monthly by the Institute for Economic Research, 3471 North Federal Highway, Fort Lauderdale, Florida 33306.

The Value Line Investment Survey is another service that investors might consider. As noted, it provides a rundown on the behavior of particular industries relative to the ups and downs of the stock market as a whole. Value Line also covers 1,700 stocks with regularity. Its rates change from time to time; in early 1982, for instance, the service offered a year's issues, fifty-two in all, for $330. The address is: The Value Line Investment Survey, 711 Third Ave., New York, New York 10017.

The Value Line service, I should add, isn't the only place where you can determine the strength of an industry's performance relative to the entire stock market during various phases of the business cycle. A. G. Becker Inc., for instance, is one of a number of securities concerns that offer similar information. Periodically, Becker issues reports containing charts showing the stock-price performance of key industries compared with the Standard & Poor's 500 index. The lines are constructed by dividing a monthly price index for a particular industry by the 500 index. Rising lines indicate outperformance, declining lines underperformance.

Finally, with regard to one's reading list, let me cautiously advise anyone wanting to dig more deeply into the crucial matter of outguessing the business cycle to obtain a copy of a large, mildly forbidding work titled *Business Cycles, Inflation and Forecasting*, by Geoffrey Moore, published by Ballinger, a subsidiary of Harper & Row, in 1980. I've intentionally left this 461-page book for last and not included it among the material clearly oriented toward business-cycle investing, since it goes far beyond the fundamentals needed for a successful investment strategy tied to the business cycle. However, if your new familiarity with the business cycle has merely whetted your appetite for more information of the subject, this exhaustive volume is for you.

Tax Talk

A word about taxes is in order. The intricacies of tax regulations, of course, are legendary. But one aspect of tax law is reasonably straightforward and highly pertinent in any do-it-yourself investment strategy geared, as this one clearly is, to the workings of the business cycle. I'm referring to capital-gains taxation.

At any time, with any investment strategy, capital-gains considerations should be weighed carefully in buy or sell decisions. If anyone tries to tell you that you shouldn't worry if you have to pay a capital-gains tax because it means you've made a successful investment, my advice is: Don't listen. I recounted in Chapter 2 how my Citibank advisers sold a variety of my long-held securities during that dreary summer of 1972 I spent in London. Their choices of what to sell—and what subsequently to buy—pained me plenty, as I've indicated. But the salt in the wounds was the fact that those stocks—Continental Oil and the others—were sold without taking capital-gains tax consequences into consideration. The Citibank people didn't even ask me what cost prices were on the stocks that they got rid of while I was overseas. In just about every instance, I had a large capital gain—one that cost me a considerable amount of extra tax dollars. When inflation is severe, of course, the capital-gains bite really can hurt—and inflation, as we know, was bad in the 1970s, particularly during that time I was in London and Citibank was selling those stocks with its discretionary power. The reason that a capital-gains tax is so particularly painful in inflationary times is, quite simply, that you often wind up paying taxes on a "gain" that really reflects nothing more than inflation, not a real increase in the value of the assets you are selling. With inflation, after paying a capital-gains tax in such a situation, you will normally find that you can't possibly duplicate what you sold—at a "gain"—for the same price.

Fortunately, the government has lately begun to wake up to how unfair—and damaging to the nation's overall investment climate—capital-gains taxation can be. The rate has been going down ever so slowly. But another thing has also been happening, and it's a matter that anyone gearing their investment strategy to the business cycle should be keenly aware of.

The length of time that an investment must be held to qualify as a long-term capital gain has grown longer. Capital gains and losses, of course, are subject to special tax regulations. A key point to keep in mind here is that a capital gain on a sale of an investment held for more than twelve months is treated by the Internal Revenue Service as a long-term capital gain. This so-called holding period has doubled in the past decade. If the investment, on the other hand, has been held for twelve months or less, any resulting gain on its sale will be treated by the IRS as a short-term capital gain. Losses on sales of investments, by the same token, are similarly defined. A loss incurred on an investment held for more than twelve months is deemed a long-term loss. A loss sustained on an investment owned for twelve months or less is considered for tax purposes a short-term loss.

In brief, twelve months is the all-important dividing line. This is important because, for example, if you do have a gain and it is only a short-term one, it will be taxed as a rule as ordinary income, at a sharply higher rate than if it were a long-term gain; the exact differential, of course, would depend on an individual's tax bracket. A short-term loss, it should be noted, also normally weighs more heavily in the tax picture. If there are no offsetting gains, under usual circumstances it can be subtracted dollar for dollar up to $3,000 from ordinary income, whereas a long-term loss may not be. Again, much may depend on the taxpayer's tax bracket.

The necessity of holding an investment for twelve months in order to qualify for long-term tax treatment obviously is a matter to be considered in an investment strategy built around fluctuations of the business cycle. It's a fact that some recessions, and even a couple of business-cycle up-phases, have lasted slightly less than twelve months. Thus, it's possible that the do-it-yourself investor who times his moves to turns in the business cycle may occasionally be compelled to take, for example, a short-term gain, which, as noted above, normally will entail a higher tax. Therefore you should weigh carefully the prospect of a higher tax against the chance that hanging on to an investment for another month or two or three—long enough for it to qualify for long-term treatment—would cause you, from a business-cycle viewpoint, to miss the boat. For example, should you sell a recently acquired stock after a recession begins even though you know that it should have been sold, say, three months before the peak of the preceding economic expansion? You may find that it would be better to wait before selling. However, my guess is that in most instances, and particularly with investments that are extrasensitive to business-cycle fluctuations, your best bet would be to stick to a basic strategy that attaches primary importance to business-cycle considerations.

I should also reemphasize that, fortunately, most business-cycle ups and downs last considerably longer than twelve months. Only ten of the twenty-nine cyclical contractions that occurred between 1854 and 1981 lasted a year or less. And only two of the corresponding expansion periods lasted a year or less. So the chances are that you won't have to concern yourself with the problem of taking, for instance, a short-term capital gain. However, be aware that the problem can arise in an abnormally short business-cycle phase.

A final word about taxes. Throughout this book, you have been urged to "do-it-yourself," to develop your own investment strategy, geared to the business cycle, and not to depend on the various establishment advisory services that would happily, for a handsome fee, manage your money for you. Given this advice to be your own investment adviser, you may now be a bit surprised to hear me say that, if there is a reasonable amount in your investment nest egg, you probably are best advised to hire an accountant to assist you with your tax returns.

Compared with the sums that many investment advisers charge, a good tax accountant is a bargain. He well may save you far more in taxes than you could possibly have saved by doing your taxes yourself. If you wind up having to pay him, say, $300, remember also that his fee is tax-deductible.

There's another plus to not doing-it-yourself when it comes to taxes. The plus has been described by Paul N. Strassels, a former tax-law specialist at the IRS and, with Robert Wool, the author of a book called *All You Need to Know About the IRS*, published by Random House in 1980. Asked once in an interview, for *U.S. News & World Report*, whether it matters if one's return is prepared by a professional tax preparer, Mr. Strassels replied:

"It doesn't matter to the computer, but it matters to the IRS auditors. They imagine you with a couple of how-to manuals opened up late on the night before deadline, and you're poring over the return, and you're the dumb, stupid taxpayer, and you're making all sorts of mistakes. But if you have a professional preparer sign that return, it's a different feeling when they look at that for the audit: 'Okay, that's questionable, but I know the firm.' IRS might want to see some sort of record to substantiate a claim, but also might think, 'We're not going to be able to pull dough out of this one that we would have if this person had prepared it himself.'"

Mr. Strassels went on to caution that he did not mean that everyone should use a professional tax preparer. He said: "Not at all. I have no qualms about people who do their own returns and feel comfortable about it. I know people who make $50,000 a year, but their financial affairs are not complex. They itemize deductions, have some dividend and interest income, maybe buy or sell a few stocks during the year. They're comfortable preparing their own return. But if you're audited, then get a tax lawyer to represent you. IRS wants it. You're defending yourself by doing it. You get two tax experts talking the same language. Your adviser can tell you: 'You made a mistake there. You can't do that.' And IRS will say: 'Fine. Now I don't have to spend all my time proving the point to this guy.' On the other hand, your adviser is going to protect your rights. He'll say: 'Don't push him around. We want this deduction. We don't have the receipt. We'll get it. We're not going to close the case out. We don't have to put up with this attitude'—that kind of thing."

This is perhaps the place to insert another, final, cautionary note of a different sort, unrelated to tax matters but central to our larger message that do-it-yourself is the best, safest, cheapest investment policy: Beware the slick appeals that establishment advisers continually produce and disseminate in efforts to lure new clients. Typical is an elegant little booklet issued in 1980 by the Private Banking Division of our old friend Citibank. Titled *On Choosing Your Investment Advisor*, it begins:

"There are thousands of stocks listed on the major exchanges and sold over-the-counter, a myriad of municipal and corporate bonds, a proliferation of money market instruments. Real estate, fine art and other tangible assets—the sheer number of investment possibilities would seem to be beyond the scope of any one advisor. Ideally, though, your advisor *should* be up-to-the minute across the spectrum of investment opportunities, able to anticipate rather than merely to react—and then to evaluate each potential investment or sale in light of the financial goals. To fulfill your needs, an investment advisor must have extraordinary qualifications. A tall order indeed."

The booklet then proceeds to state modestly that you should consider, to fill this "tall order," the "qualifications" of bankers attached to Citibank's Private Banking Division, or PBD, as it's called within the bank. These individuals, the booklet goes on, offer:

"1. Experience. Your PBD Banker works *only* with individuals, but can call upon the experience of Citibank, one of the largest investment managers in the United States.

"2. Information. Your PBD Banker has immediate access to Citibank's worldwide information network for trends, market factors, economic insights, forecasts, research data.

"3. People. Your PBD Banker is a highly trained officer of Citibank, a 'general practitioner' of financial management through whom you can get the help of specialists in every financial discipline—of professionals in taxation, estates, trusts, real estate, to name a few.

"4. Objectivity. Your PBD Banker has no axe to grind for any one kind of investment, no pat answers, no one-size-fits-all philosophy. The counselor you get fits you and you alone.

"5. Perspective. Your PBD Banker's familiarity with your whole financial picture gives him, or her, a valuable overview. Thus, investments are not considered in a vacuum, but in relation to your goals."

The pitch continues: "As an investment advisor, your PBD Banker does have extraordinary qualifications."

The booklet finally urges that "if you share the popular notion that banks manage investments with extreme conservatism and within a rigidly limited number of options, you'll be pleasantly surprised. True, Private Banking Division's underlying philosophy stresses preservation and protection of your money. By its very nature, this philosophy aims for steady growth. And prudent risk gets due consideration as you will see."

Such appeals may sound enticing indeed. But the only way to be certain that you'll be "pleasantly surprised" and not unpleasantly surprised, as I was back in 1972, is to do the job yourself. It's a job, I submit, that's far less forbidding than generally supposed. And one that is bound to produce, with a little effort and thanks to the business cycle, a delightfully large number of very pleasant surprises.

INDEX

Agricultural products, 170–72, 173
Allied Corp., 111
All You Need to Know About the IRS (Strassels and Wool), 199
Aluminum Co. of America, 44–45, 111
Amax Inc., 7, 10, 12, 14
American Brands, 111
American Can, 111
American economy. *See* Economy
American Institute Counselors Inc., 173
American Metal Climax Inc. *See* Amax Inc.
American Numismatic Association, 163
American Stock Exchange, 105, 161
American Telephone & Telegraph Co., 6, 10, 12, 32, 111
Amherst College Endowment Fund, 32–33
Ammidon, Hoyt, 19, 21
Annual reports, 123, 138–39
Apparel manufacture, 116
Arbitrage, 189
Area Redeployment Act (1961), 63
Argus Research Corp., 42, 143
Austrian hundred-corona bullion coin, 163
Automobile manufacturing stocks, 117, 118
Automobile repair, 134
Avon Products Inc., 6, 10, 11, 12, 15, 16, 22, 27, 49, 55, 57

Bache Halsey Stuart Shield, 168–89
Bank of England, 34
Bank of New York, 38, 39
Barron's (weekly), 16, 38, 46, 193
BCD (*Business Conditions Digest*), 78, 82, 85–89, 94, 98, 100, 102, 113, 115, 117, 127, 158, 170, 174, 177, 178, 181, 183, 193
Becker, A. G., Inc., 195
Benny, Jack, 19

Bernstein, Sanford C., & Co., 96
Bethlehem Steel Corp., 19, 111
Bleiberg, Robert M., 46
Blyth Eastman Dillon & Co., 40
Blyvooruitzicht, 39
Bondholder, 150
Bonds, 56, 103, 141, 142, 160
Books, rare, 160
Boom, 5
Borch, Fred J., 20, 21
Borowski, Irwin, 48
Bretton Woods system, 31
Bristol-Myers Co., 122, 123
Britain, 61
British pound devaluation, 28, 31, 34
Brown Brothers Harriman, 41
Building industry stocks, 115–16, 118
Building permits, 89, 92, 93, 94, 109, 115, 182, 183, 184
Bullion coins, 163
Bureau of Labor Statistics, 54, 97
Burns, Arthur F., 63–65, 66–67, 190
Business confidence survey, 43, 53
Business cycle, 31, 50, 51, 55–57, 58, 59, 77–83, 84–102, 124–25, 187–88
 contraction, 79, 187
 expansion, 5, 11, 51, 79, 85, 90, 187
 fixed income investment, 142–48
 gold prices, 160, 164, 165
 inflation. *See* Inflation
 noncyclical factors, 134
 peaks, 7–9, 83, 88, 106, 187, 188
 silver prices, 167
 stock behavior and, 120–21
 stock prices and, 105–9, 110
 troughs, 80, 83, 88, 106, 187, 188
Business Cycle Developments (BCD), 78
Business Cycle in a Changing World, The (Burns), 190
Business Cycle Indicators, 190
Business Cycles, Inflation and Forecasting (Moore), 195–96

Business Week magazine, 45, 46, 137, 192, 193

Call, 137, 189
Capital consumption allowance (CCA), 53
Capital-equipment business, 180
Capital-gains tax, 56, 196–98
Capital spending, 117, 118, 119
Carter, James, 132
Cash, 57, 178, 179, 180
Cattle cycle, 170–71
CBS Inc., 45
Cement industry, 118–19
Center for International Business Cycle Research, 189
Ceramics, Chinese, 160
Certificates of deposit, 195
Chicago Federal Reserve Bank, 171
Chicago Tribune Co., 20
Citibank, 7–11, 12, 13, 15, 16, 17, 22, 24, 25, 26, 27, 30, 47, 49, 50, 51, 55, 56, 57, 171, 196, 200–1
  discretionary management power over clients' investments, 8–9
Citicorp, 20
Cohen, Morris, 45
Coincident indicators, 80, 83, 100, 104, 116, 117, 118, 174, 177, 180, 188
Coins, 160, 163
Collectibles, 172–73
Collecting Tomorrow's Collectibles (Feinman), 193
Commerce Department, 43, 52, 53, 54, 55, 77, 82, 85, 88, 94, 100, 110, 174
Commercial paper, 195
Commodities/commodity markets, 57, 158–60, 173, 192
Commodity tax straddles, 137
Common stock, 130, 131, 133
"Composite Index of Leading Economic Indicators," 52, 55
Conference Board, 43, 45, 189
Conoco Inc. *See* Continental Oil Co.
Consumer price index, 62, 84, 85, 96–97, 160
Consumer sentiment index, 89
Consumer spending, 80, 117–18
Continental Oil Co., 6, 10, 12, 13, 56
Continental Telephone Corp., 10, 11, 12, 13, 49, 55
Contraction, 79, 187
Copper prices, 167–68
Corporate bonds, 144, 146, 147, 148, 153
Corporate profits, 50, 51, 52
"Corporate Profits After Taxes with IVA and CCA," 53
Council of Economic Advisers, 77
Credentials, 40–41
Credit, 25
Currency, 37, 127, 158
Curtis, Tony, 19
Cycles (Stokes), 191

Data Resources Inc., 77
Davis, Polk & Wardwell, 20
Debevoise, Plimpton, Lyons & Gates, 20
Debt, 25, 67–70
Democratic party, 133
Depression, 5, 187
Diamonds, 160
Discount Brokerage, 138
Diversified operations, 122
Dominick & Dominick Inc., 31, 32, 33, 34
Double top reversals, 134
Dow Jones & Co., 16
Dow Jones industrial stock average, 9, 37–38, 44, 94, 107, 108, 109, 110, 111, 133, 135, 136
Downticks, 189
Dreman, David N., 16, 17
Dreyfus, 149
Dun & Bradstreet Corp., 43
Dunaway, Faye, 19
Duncan indicator, 189
Du Pont, 6, 32, 111, 139

Eastman Kodak, 112
Eckstein, Otto, 77, 78
Economic Calendar, 193, 194
Economic indicators. *See* Coincident indicators; Lagging indicators; Leading indicators
Economist, The (London), 193
Economists, 24, 26, 27, 28, 29
Economy, 3, 4, 5, 11, 31, 50, 51, 77, 79, 81, 85, 89–90
Emergency Employment Act (1971), 64
Employment, 5, 50–51, 63–64, 181
Employment Act (1946), 63
Eurodollars, 195
Expansion, 5, 11, 51, 79, 85, 90, 187
Exter, John, 23, 24–27, 37, 40
Exxon Corp., 7, 10, 12, 13, 45, 112

Farmland, 160
Farrow, Mia, 19
Federal funds, 195
Federal Reserve Bank of Richmond, 193, 195
Federal Reserve banks, 70, 155, 171, 193, 195
Federal Reserve Board, 63, 66, 97, 190
Federal Reserve system, 24, 25, 26, 41, 155, 156, 192
  easy money policy, 31
Feinman, Jeffrey, 193
Fiske, Robert B., Jr., 20
Fitch Investors Service, 151, 153
Fixed-income investment, 140–56, 175
  and business cycle, 142–48
  and inflation, 148–51
  taxation, 153–54
  unfixed issues, 154–55
Flynn, Perry, 49–50, 52, 54, 58, 160
Forbes (magazine), 173, 193

INDEX

Ford, Gerald, 132
Foreign exchange, 7, 160
Foreign investment, 126–29, 189
Foreign trade, 70–71
Forest-products stocks, 119
Fortune (magazine), 42
Foy, Lewis W., 19

Gates, Thomas S., Jr., 20
General Electric Co., 20, 21, 112, 121–22
General Foods, 112
General Motors, 32, 112, 121, 176, 178, 179
Germany, 65–66
Glossary—The Language of Investing (booklet), 189
Gold bars, 162
Gold bullion, 162
Gold futures, 164–65
Goldman, Sachs & Co., 44, 100
Gold-mining stocks, 25, 26, 31, 34–36, 37–40, 57, 160
Gold prices, 160, 164, 165
Gold tangibles, 160–65
Goodyear, 112
Grace, Peter, 68–69
Grace, W. R., & Co., 68
Granville, Joseph E., 135–37
Granville Market Letter, 135–37
Grayson, Charles, 42
Great Depression, 63, 64, 68, 73, 107, 175
Gross national product (GNP), 50, 51, 70, 80, 83
Growth stocks, 10, 11, 12, 13, 16, 58
Gulag Archipelago, The (Solzhenitsyn), 71
Gulf & Western Industries, 122

Hartebeestfontein, 39
Harwood, Edward C., 47, 173
Hayden, Stone & Co., 30
Health care, 134
Health insurance, 134
Hecht, Sanford D., 103
Herzig, Paul, 34–36
Herzig, P. R., & Co., 34–36
Home-appliance industry, 118
Homestake Mining Company, 161
Home-Stake Production Co., 18–22, 47
Housing, 160, 182
"How to Play the Options Game," 137
How to Read a Financial Statement, 193
Hutton, E. F., 138
Hypothecation, 189

Inco, 112
Indicators of Business Expansions and Contractions, 190
Industrial production, 80, 182, 183
Inflation, 5, 57, 59–65, 94–97, 110–11, 130, 131, 148–51, 175
Ingersoll-Rand, 178, 180, 183
Institute for Economic Research, 195
Instruments of the Money Market (booklet), 193, 195

Interest rates, 25, 26, 31, 32, 33
  and fixed income securities, 142
  and inflation, 130, 131
  long term, 143, 144
  short term, 143, 147
Internal Revenue Service (IRS), 197, 199, 200
International Business Machines (IBM), 10, 11, 12, 13, 49, 55, 112
International Harvester, 112
International Monetary Fund, 66
International money system, 24, 25, 28, 31
International Paper, 112
Inventory valuation adjustment (IVA), 53
Inverse head and shoulders reversals, 134
Investigative reporting, 18, 19
Investment/investing, 1, 21, 22, 23, 103–4, 109
  do-it-yourself techniques, 4
  geared to business cycle, 5
  rules, 2–3
Investment literature, 190–95

Japan, 61, 127, 128
Johns-Manville, 112
Johnson, Lyndon B., 77

Kajutti, Brian D., 94
Kendall, Donald M., 20
Keynes, John Maynard, 63
Kondratieff, Nicolai Dimitrievich, 71–72
Kondratieff wave, 71–75
Kondratieff Wave, The (Shuman and Rosenau), 191
Kuznets, Simon, 75
Kuznets cycles, 75

Lagging indicators, 100, 104, 113, 116, 118, 164, 167, 174, 177, 188
Lawrence, Cyrus J., Inc., 44
Leading indicators, 83, 84, 85, 86, 87, 88, 89, 116, 158, 174, 188
  composite index, 88, 90–92, 104, 189
Lindsay, George N., 20
Lindsay, John V., 20
Liquid assets, 89
Long-term trends, 127, 130, 132
Lumber prices, 169

Machine tool industry, 113–15, 118, 126
McClintick, Dave, 18, 19, 21, 22
McElroy, Neil H., 20
McFall, Russell W., 20
Macy, R. H., & Co., 20
Mahoney, David J., Jr., 20
Manpower Development and Training Act (1962), 63–64
Manufacturers Hanover Trust, 43
Manufacturing industries, 88, 89
Margin calls, 189
Matthau, Walter, 19

Merck, 112
Merrill Lynch & Co. (Merrill Lynch, Pierce, Fenner & Smith), 27, 28, 34, 138, 149, 193
Metals investing, 168–69
Mexican fifty-peso bullion coin, 163
Millionaires, 1–2
Minnesota Mining & Manufacturing, 112
Molloy, Ernest L., 20
Money Market Fund Safety Ratings, 195
Money-market mutual funds, 149
Money supply, 89, 97–99, 104, 182, 183, 184
Moody's Investors Services, 151, 153
Moore, Geoffrey H., 189, 190, 195
Moore, George S., 20
Morgan Guaranty Trust Co., 20
Municipal bonds, 26, 144, 146

National Bureau of Economic Research, 55, 79–80, 83, 107, 176, 190
National City Bank of New York. *See* Citibank
NCR Corp., 20
New York Federal Reserve Bank, 70, 155
New York Stock Exchange, 12, 20, 105, 127, 138, 161, 189
New York *Times*, 88, 90, 193
Nimitz, Chester W., Jr., 20
Norton Simon Inc., 20
Notes, 142
Numismatic premium, 163
Numismatics, 163–64

Odd lots, 189
Oelman, Robert S., 20
Oil/gas drilling operations, 19, 20, 21–22
Oil prices, 11, 61, 81–82, 160, 165
Oil stock companies, 165
Old masters, 160
On Choosing Your Investment Advisor (booklet), 200–1
Over-the-counter stocks, 105
Owens-Illinois, 112

Paine Webber, 138
Parks, Robert H., 40–41
Peaks, 79, 83, 88, 106, 187, 188
PepsiCo Inc., 20
Perkin-Elmer Corp., 20
Personal consumption, 111
Personal income, 80, 125–26, 181
Plant and equipment spending, 113–15, 117
Politics, 132–33
Price-earnings ratio, 16–17
Procter & Gamble Co., 20, 112
Public Service Company of New Mexico, 130–32
Public utilities, 60, 67, 130–32, 176
Public Works Acceleration Act (1962), 63
Pulitzer Prize, 19, 21
Put, 137, 189

Quick & Reilly, 138

Ratio, 100–2, 104, 177, 183
Real-estate investing, 57, 103
Recession, 5, 28, 43, 45, 59, 60, 71, 73, 79, 82, 85, 110, 111, 187
  1948–49, 96
  1953–54, 90, 96
  1957–58, 90, 96
  1960–61, 90, 96, 115
  1969–70, 52, 90, 96, 98, 109, 115
  1973–75, 11, 53, 57, 73, 81, 90, 96, 109, 114, 116, 117, 118, 119, 124, 130, 143, 144, 171, 175
  1980, 88, 92, 110, 143
Recovery, 5, 59, 60, 71, 79, 85, 88, 90, 187
  1954, 92
  1958, 92
  1961, 92, 124
  1970, 92
  1975, 92
Regan, Donald T., 28
Relative strength index, 114, 116, 118–19
Republican party, 133
Repurchase agreements, 195
Retail-store stocks, 117
Retirement community market, 182
Roosa, Robert, 41
Roosevelt, Franklin D., 163
Rosenau, David, 191
Rustin, Dick, 18
Rutgers University, 189

Salomon Brothers, 150, 165
Samuelson, Paul, 26
Schroeder, Naess & Thomas, 45
Schultz, Harry D., 40–42
Schwab, Charles, 138
Sears, Roebuck & Co., 10, 11, 12, 13, 49, 55, 57, 112, 183
Secular developments, 59–61
Securities and Exchange Commission (SEC), 47, 48
Security ratings, 151–53
Seligman, Eustace, 33
Service industries, 133–35
Shea, William A., 20
Shearson, 138
Shepley, James R., 20
Shilling, A. Gary, 23, 27–30, 34, 37, 40, 69
Shiskin, Julius, 190
Shuman, James B., 191
Siebert, Muriel, 20
Siff, Oakley and Marks Inc., 68
Silver prices, 167
Silver tangibles, 160, 166–67
Smiley, Donald B., 20
Solzhenitsyn, Alexander I., 71
Somers, Albert T., 45
South African kruggerand bullion coin, 163
Southland Corp., 10, 11, 12, 13, 49, 55

INDEX

Spencer, William I., 20
"Spot-market Prices, Raw Materials," 158
Stalin, Joseph, 71
Stamps, 160
Standard & Poor's Corp., 151–53
Standard & Poor's industrial index, 12, 55, 56, 94, 96, 97, 98, 104, 107, 110, 127, 150, 175, 176, 177, 179, 180, 184, 195
Standard Oil of California, 6, 10, 12, 13, 56, 112
Standard Oil of New Jersey. *See* Exxon Corp.
Statistical series, 85, 88, 89
Stealing from the Rich: The Home-Stake Oil Swindle (McClintick), 19
Stockbrokers, 138–39
Stockholder, 140, 150
Stock market, 11, 24–25, 31, 37, 52, 53, 55, 103–12, 113–23, 153, 160
 new stock issues, 105, 130–31
 stock behavior and, 120–21
 technical analysis, 134, 135–37
Stock-option trading, 136–37
Stock-price index, 94–97
Stock prices, 52, 55, 56, 89, 105–9, 110, 127–29
"Stock Prices and Business Cycles" table, 105–9
Stock(s), 103, 113–23
 assessing value, 16
 fitting into industry, 121
 growth, 10, 11, 12, 13, 16, 58
 new issues, 105, 130–31
 price-earnings ratio, 16–17
Stokes, Dick A., 19
Stop-loss orders, 173
Stout, Gardner, 31, 32
Stout, Varick, 31, 33
Strassels, Paul N., 199–200
Streisand, Barbra, 19
Sullivan & Cromwell, 33
Sunshine Mining Co., 155
Survey Research Center, University of Michigan, 89

Tangible assets, 103, 157–73
Tax accountant, 199
Taxation, 196–200
 capital gain, 56, 196–98
 commodity tax straddle, 137
 fixed-income securities, 153–54
Tax shelters, 21
Technical analysis investing, 134, 135–37
Teele, Stanley, 32–33
Tehan, William, 23, 30–36, 37, 39, 40, 58
Telecommunications, 134
Texaco, 112
Texas Instruments, 45
Time Inc., 20
Timing, 109
Train, John, 173

Treasury bills, 37, 57, 142, 143, 144, 145, 148, 149, 155, 195
Treasury bonds, 146, 155
Treasury notes, 155
Troughs, 80, 83, 88, 106, 187, 188
Truck manufacturing stocks, 117
Trucks, 117
Twenty-nine Industries (table), 120–21, 130

Unemployment, 84, 85, 182, 183, 187, 189
Union Carbide, 112
United States Government
 balance of payments deficit, 31, 32, 33
 debt, 68–69
 Department of Commerce. *See* Commerce Department
 employment legislation, 63–64
 federal funds, 195
 gross national product (GNP), 50, 51, 70, 80, 83
 investment protective regulations, 47–48
 number of individuals depending for income on, 69
 savings bonds, 46
 Treasury bills, 37, 57, 142, 143, 144, 145, 148, 195
 Treasury bonds, 146, 155
 Treasury Department, 155–56
 Treasury notes, 155
U. S. Home, 182, 184
U.S. News & World Report, 199
U. S. Steel, 112
United States Trust Co., 1, 19, 21
United Technologies, 112
University of Michigan, Consumer Research Center, 89
Upticks, 189

Value Line Investment Survey, 114, 116, 118–19, 180, 183, 195
Vietnam, 175
Volcker, Paul A., 66

Wall Street Journal, The, 15, 18, 21, 26, 38, 39, 47, 88, 89, 90, 97, 102, 149, 155, 174, 175, 177, 181, 192, 193
Walters, Barbara, 19
West Dreifontein, 39
Western Union Corp., 20
West Germany, 61, 127, 128
Westinghouse Electric, 112
White, Weld & Co., 29, 34
Winters, Jonathan, 19
Wisconsin Electric Power, 6, 10, 12, 14
Wojnilower, Albert M., 39
Wood, J. Howard, 20
Wool, Robert, 199
Woolworth, 112
World War II, 63
Wriston, Walter B., 20

Zaire, 169